Tourism Disrupted

How Elitism and Third-World Models
Shape the Northern Mariana Islands

By
Tatiana A. Babauta

Copyright © 2023 Tatiana Babauta
All rights reserved.

All rights reserved. This book contains material protected under International and Federal Copyright Laws and Treaties. Any unauthorized reprint or use of this material is prohibited. No part of this book may be reproduced or transmitted in any form or by any means, electronic or mechanical, including photocopying, recording, or by any information storage and retrieval system without express written permission from the author/publisher.

ISBN: 979-8-218-35409-1

Dedication

This book is lovingly dedicated to the pillars of my life:

To my beloved husband, your love and support have been my unwavering anchor in life's vast and often tumultuous ocean. Your strength, wisdom, and unfailing companionship have provided solace and been instrumental in forging the path of this incredible journey. Each step, decision, and moment of doubt was met with your encouraging words and understanding heart, turning the pages of this book and our lives into a beautiful reality.

To my mom, who is a cornerstone of wisdom and grace in my life. Your insights and values have been instrumental in shaping who I am today, influencing my thoughts and the words I share. Your lessons in resilience, compassion, and integrity have been invaluable. The wisdom you have imparted is deeply embedded in the fabric of this book, with each lesson you have taught subtly influencing its narrative and my journey. Every page of this book is imbued with your voice, teachings, and the unconditional love you have always shown me.

To Elizabeth and Dylan, my dearest children, whose sharp intellect and boundless curiosity are a constant source of awe. Your enthusiasm for life and learning illuminate every corner of our world. You turn every challenge into an adventure and every success into a shared celebration. Seeing you both grow, absorb knowledge, and approach the world with such open and eager hearts has been an incredible source of happiness for me. It amazes me every day how you both take on life with such smart curiosity and sheer delight. This approach of yours not only fills me with hope for the bright future you have ahead and inspires me in more ways than I could have ever imagined. This book reflects the dreams and hopes I harbor for you in a world that eagerly awaits your contributions and discoveries.

To my family in the Commonwealth of the Northern Mariana Islands: Each of you has been a pillar of support and joy in my life. Your strength and warmth have embraced me and instilled a sense of hope and possibility that permeates this book. In your embrace, I have seen a world where tradition harmonizes with aspirations for a better tomorrow, shaping our journey toward a brighter future.

To my friends in the Commonwealth of the Northern Mariana Islands: You have been the architects of unforgettable memories and invaluable lessons. In your company, I have experienced the true heart of the islands — a unique blend of hospitality, generosity, and enduring bonds. This book reflects our shared experiences, echoing the optimism and friendship you have so generously shared with me, fueling our collective dreams for a future filled with progress and joy.

Introduction

In the Western Pacific, a string of islands offers a stark contrast of experiences. Their shimmering waters and sunlit shores present a beautiful facade, but a more complex reality lies beneath them. The Commonwealth of the Northern Mariana Islands (CNMI) represents not just a tropical idyll but a locale where the serenity of nature is juxtaposed with intricate socio-economic issues. This is the CNMI, a microcosm of global diversity, a place where the enchanting allure of tourism grapples with the shadows of elitism and the remnants of third-world structures.

As the pages of "Tourism Disrupted: How Elitism and Third-World Models Shape the Northern Mariana Islands" unfold, we venture into an intricate world. This book is not merely a chronicle of the islands' tourism industry but a deep dive into the socio-economic transformation triggered by this industry. We explore how a region, often overshadowed by more famous destinations, navigates the turbulent waters of global tourism, carving out an identity uniquely its own.

This journey takes us across the varied terrains of the Mariana Archipelago. We navigate from Saipan's lively streets to Tinian's tranquil shores, through Rota's undulating landscapes, and into the pristine wilderness of the Northern Islands. Here, we discover a world that stands apart from the usual routes of popular tourism destinations. In these islands, the tourism narrative unfolds in complex layers, each revealing the paradox of beauty and challenge.

Here, in the CNMI, the dual impact of elitism and third-world frameworks on tourism development becomes evident. The islands face a balancing act in pursuing economic growth through tourism.

They navigate the contrasting forces of their stunning natural beauty and the socio-economic realities that challenge their progress. This paradox creates a fascinating yet formidable landscape for stakeholders in the tourism industry.

Nevertheless, the story of CNMI's tourism is not just about challenges but also immense potential and opportunities. It is a narrative of change and empowerment, where grassroots initiatives play a pivotal role in steering the course of the tourism industry. The book delves into these undercurrents of transformation, celebrating the efforts of individuals, communities, and organizations determined to foster a more sustainable and equitable tourism sector.

As the discussion evolves, we examine the transformative power of technology, the critical intersection of climate change and tourism, and the prospects for diversifying the CNMI's economy beyond the confines of tourism. Interwoven in these discussions are the social impacts of tourism, destination branding, and the powerful yet often overlooked role of cultural heritage.

"Tourism Disrupted: How Elitism and Third-World Models Shape the Northern Mariana Islands" transcends typical analytical discourse, offering a rich narrative that informs, inspires, and urges change. It stands as a tribute to the enduring spirit and adaptability of the Northern Mariana Islands. This narrative delves deep into how these islands are reshaping their role in international tourism, all while fiercely guarding their distinct cultural heritage.

In its final analysis, the book not only narrates the present but also charts a course for the future of the CNMI's tourism industry. It lays the groundwork for discussions and actions crucial in the ever-evolving world of tourism. Join us on this fascinating journey of exploration and discovery, where the untold story of the Commonwealth of the Northern Mariana Islands offers profound insights and a revitalized perspective on the intricate dynamics of global tourism.

Table of Contents

Chapter 1: Emergence of Elitism: The Historical Context............ 10

Chapter 2: Understanding Third World Frameworks: From Colonialism to Dependency 17

Chapter 3: The Northern Mariana Islands: An Overlooked Paradise.. 28

Chapter 4: Establishment of Tourism in the CNMI...................... 35

Chapter 5: Influence of the Island's Elite on the Tourism Industry... 39

Chapter 6: Impact of Third-World Frameworks on Tourism Development 49

Chapter 7: There is No Balance Between Third World Frameworks and Sustainable Tourism 62

Chapter 8: Decolonizing Tourism: Breaking Away from Elitist Paradigms 73

Chapter 9: Evaluating the TRIP Initiative: A Critical Analysis of CNMI's Multimillion-Dollar Tourism Strategy and Its Economic Implications.. 86

Chapter 10: Impact of Digital Evolution and Technological Innovation on Tourism.. 93

Chapter 11: Unseen Battles and Debates: The Undercurrents of Tourism 104

Chapter 12: Climate Change and Tourism: An Unavoidable Intersection 114

Chapter 13: Policy and Governance: Steering the Course of Tourism Development in the CNMI...................................... 126

Chapter 14: Social Impact of Diverse Tourism Types 139

Chapter 15: Opportunities for Change: Empowerment and Grassroots Initiatives 151

Chapter 16: Reimagining Local Participation: From Spectators to Beneficiaries 165

Chapter 17: Economic Diversification: Beyond The Tourism Industry 174

Chapter 18: Destination Rebranding and Marketing: Crafting the CNMI Image 186

Chapter 19: Unleashing the Potential of Cultural Heritage in Tourism 201

Chapter 20: A New Horizon: Shaping a Sustainable and Equitable Future for CNMI Tourism 212

References 215

Chapter 1

Emergence of Elitism: The Historical Context

The Northern Mariana Islands' contemporary tourism sector is profoundly shaped by its rich history, especially the rise and development of elitism throughout various eras. By navigating the intricate pathways of its colonial past, global interactions, and changing socio-economic scenarios, this chapter seeks to clarify the structural foundation of elitism deeply embedded in the islands' tourism landscape. By examining this historical context, we gain a deeper understanding of the current dynamics shaping the tourism sector in the Northern Mariana Islands.

The Northern Mariana Islands, comprising 14 islands in the Western Pacific, possess a rich and tumultuous history shaped by various colonial powers. From the indigenous Chamorro and Carolinian people's initial settlement, successive Spanish, German, Japanese, and American dominations have left enduring marks on the island's culture, economy, and social structure. This continuous colonization created a stratified society, with the islands' colonizers often occupying positions of power and wealth.

The period of Spanish dominance, from the 17th to the 19th century, has marked a crucial chapter in the historical narrative of the Northern Mariana Islands (Foster & Ballendorf, 2023). This time frame laid the foundational socio-political dynamics that would influence the archipelago for future generations. Spanish Crown viewed the islands as a strategic outpost in the vast Pacific and a fertile ground for spreading Christianity (Foster & Ballendorf, 2023). This dual objective of strategic control and religious conversion played a pivotal role in the emergence of elitism in the islands.

As the Spanish galleons sailed into the pristine waters of the Mariana Islands, they brought with them not only their military might but also their socio-cultural ethos. The Spanish Crown's primary objective was establishing a stronghold in the Pacific, a waypoint for their Manila-Acapulco galleon trade (Tan, 2020). With their strategic location, the islands provided the perfect stopover for these trading vessels. However, beyond the economic interests, the Spanish were driven by a fervent desire to convert the indigenous population to Christianity.

The establishment of missions and churches became a common sight across the islands. With the backing of the colonial administration, Spanish friars embarked on a zealous campaign to convert the Chamorro and Carolinian populations. While the spread of Christianity had its merits, bringing education and healthcare advancements, it also became a tool for control (Heath, 1975) (Hezel, 1988). The indigenous belief systems were often sidelined or suppressed, and the local populace was encouraged, often forcefully, to adopt Spanish customs, traditions, and religious practices.

This religious endeavor further entrenched societal divisions. The Spanish clergy and officials, with their European lineage, naturally positioned themselves at the top of this hierarchy. They controlled the political and economic levers and held spiritual authority. The indigenous people, on the other hand, found themselves at the lower rungs, their societal status diminished by the very fact of their indigenous identity. In their bid to 'civilize' the islands, the Spanish inadvertently created a class of elites who enjoyed privileges and powers denied to the native inhabitants.

Furthermore, the Spanish introduced the encomienda system, a feudal-like structure where certain colonists were granted authority over specific regions and their inhabitants. These encomenderos, as they were called, had the right to extract labor and tribute from the local population. In return, they were expected to provide protection and Christian education. However, in practice, this system often led to exploitation, with the encomenderos amassing wealth and power at the expense of the indigenous people (Britannica, 2022).

As the Spanish influence began to wane in the Northern Mariana Islands, a new chapter unfolded with the arrival of the Germans. This transition was not just a change of flags but a shift in the fabric of elitism and power dynamics established over centuries.

The end of the 19th century saw Spain's grip on its global territories loosen. The aftermath of the Spanish-American War led to Spain selling the Northern Mariana Islands to Germany in 1899 (Farrell, 1991). While the Spanish era was characterized by religious fervor and cultural assimilation, the German period brought a more pragmatic and economic-driven approach.

Germany's primary interest in the islands was economic. They saw potential in the islands' agricultural resources, particularly copra production (Ballendorf & Foster, 2021). This focus on commerce and trade led to the establishment of large plantations. Moreover, with these plantations came a new class of elites: German plantation owners and traders. These individuals, backed by the German colonial administration, became the new power centers, controlling significant portions of the islands' economy.

The German administration's approach was methodical and structured. They introduced modern agricultural techniques, built infrastructure, and sought to make the islands a thriving economic hub (Farrell, 1991). While beneficial in many ways, this modernization also deepened the class divides. The Chamorro and Carolinian populations, who once held positions of relative autonomy during the Spanish era, were now often relegated to roles as laborers on German-owned plantations.

Education under German rule took a utilitarian turn. The focus shifted to vocational training to produce skilled laborers for the colony's economic machinery (NMI Museum, 2023). This approach, while pragmatic, further solidified the societal hierarchy. Those who controlled the means of production and trade—primarily the German settlers and businessmen—were at the top, while the indigenous populations served this economic engine.

The German administration instilled a sense of order and structure with its bureaucratic efficiency. Unlike the Spanish, the Germans did not prioritize cultural assimilation or religious conversion. Instead, their primary goal was to maximize economic output, which created a distinct class of elites and reshaped the societal dynamics of the islands. While modernization occurred during this period, it also deepened the divides between the powerful and the marginalized, leaving a lasting impact on the social structure of the islands.

Following the German era, the Northern Mariana Islands came under the influence of Japan. As the world moved through the 20th century, Japan was extending its reach, and soon enough, the League of Nations gave them control over the Northern Marianas (Ballendorf & Foster, 2021). This was not just a change in leadership but a new twist in the islands' ongoing saga of social hierarchies and elitism.

Japan had a two-pronged plan for the Marianas. They saw the islands as military assets and economic goldmines, particularly for fishing, farming, and sugar production (Ballendorf & Foster, 2021).

This dual ambition led to some real upgrades in infrastructure and the economy but also set the stage for a new social pecking order.

Japanese families and businesses started moving in, often with the backing of big corporations or the government itself. They set up shop, literally and figuratively, taking control of the islands' emerging industries like sugar cane farming and fishing. The Japanese involvement was more than just economic; it was a strategic move to establish dominance and position themselves at the forefront of the social hierarchy.

For the native Chamorro and Carolinian populations, these events echoed past experiences, creating a sense of repetition in their historical narrative. They had been down this road before with the Spanish and the Germans. Under Japanese rule, they found themselves pushed to the margins once again. They were part of this new economy but often, as laborers, stuck in roles that offered little room for growth. With their newfound economic and administrative clout, the Japanese became the latest elite class, adding another chapter to the islands' long history of social divides.

On the cultural front, the Japanese era was a mix of blending and standing apart. Japanese schools were opened, Shinto shrines became part of the local scenery, and Japanese festivals added new colors to the islands' cultural palette. While the Japanese did not force their culture on the locals, they promoted it, adding another layer to their elite status.

However, let us not forget that the Japanese era was not about social divides. The islands saw real improvements in roads, healthcare, and schools (Farrell, 1991). The economic boom, driven by the Japanese, had some trickle-down effects, making life better for the locals, even if they were often in the back seat.

The Japanese era was another critical episode in the Northern Mariana Islands' ongoing story of colonialism and social hierarchies. The Japanese, wielding their economic and cultural influence, became the new top dogs, continuing a pattern set by those who came before them.

Following World War II, the Northern Mariana Islands entered a new phase under the stewardship of the United States. This transition brought notable changes in the islands' governance and reshaped their socio-political environment. This change was not just about a new administration but a shift in the islands' political and societal dynamics. The U.S. introduced democratic principles, reshaping the governance of the islands. However, with this new system, a fresh form of elitism emerged. Local political figures began to rise, wielding significant control over the islands' resources and power dynamics.

In this era, the narrative of the Northern Mariana Islands intertwined with the broader context of global politics. The heightening of the Cold War, marked by the stark rivalry between the United States and the Soviet Union, significantly influenced worldwide geopolitical interactions. The Pacific region emerged as a critical arena in this geopolitical chess game, with both superpowers scouting for strategic advantages. Situated at a key strategic point (2023), the Northern Mariana Islands found themselves at the heart of this international power struggle. Their location became invaluable to the United States as a prime stage for demonstrating American military strength in the Pacific.

In 1975, the bond between the United States and the Northern Mariana Islands was significantly strengthened by signing the Covenant (CNMI, 2023). This pivotal agreement marked the islands' transformation into a Commonwealth under the United States, drawing them more intimately into the American sphere. This association provided the islands with economic support and security and created economic dependency. The U.S. influence increased the inflow of external resources, leading to the growth of another local elite class involved in tourism and related industries.

The amalgamation of these historical, socio-economic, and global factors has created an elitist framework that is now deeply intertwined with the contemporary tourism industry. Crucially, this elitism is not just a vestige of history; it remains a dynamic force in the current era, actively swaying decision-making, molding policies, and impacting the lives of the local community.

Tracing the myriad influences and shifts in power dynamics, the Northern Mariana Islands have witnessed the evolution of a distinct elitist framework that intertwines with its modern tourism industry. This intricate history mosaic reflects the remnants of bygone eras and actively shapes the present socio-economic landscape. To fully appreciate the tourism narrative of the Northern Mariana Islands, it is paramount to understand its historical roots of elitism, which will set the stage for subsequent examinations of its ongoing implications in the broader context of third-world tourism dynamics.

Chapter 2

Understanding Third World Frameworks: From Colonialism to Dependency

This chapter explores the intricate and often overlooked narratives that have shaped the tourism industry in the CNMI. Third-world frameworks, colonialism, and dependency concepts are at the heart of this exploration – each playing a pivotal role in molding the socio-economic fabric of the CNMI and its tourism sector. Our journey through this chapter seeks to unravel these complex layers, offering insights into how historical and global economic narratives have influenced the islands' current tourism landscape.

The term "Third World," originating during the Cold War era, initially denoted countries not aligned with either NATO (the 'First World') or the Communist Bloc (the 'Second World'). Over time, however, this terminology has evolved, shedding its political connotations and transforming into a descriptor for nations grappling with socio-economic underdevelopment, often marked by challenges such as poverty, limited industrialization, and economic dependency (Banton, 2022). This chapter recognizes that the usage of "Third World" has been criticized and has decreased in favor of academic and political discourse due to its derogatory implications. Nonetheless, it serves as a critical lens to view the global disparities and structural inequities that continue to impact many regions, including the CNMI.

In the context of the CNMI, the legacy of colonialism and the ensuing dependency dynamics are instrumental in understanding the evolution of its tourism industry. The islands' history of being ruled by Spanish, German, Japanese, and American powers has left a rich cultural tapestry and a legacy of economic and social structures that significantly affect its present and future. This chapter intends to thoroughly investigate these historical roots, scrutinizing how colonial influences reshaped traditional socio-economic systems, leading to a lasting dependency that persistently shapes the tourism dynamics of the islands.

We embark on a historical journey through the CNMI, connecting the theoretical underpinnings of colonialism and the early stages of economic dependency with the specific events and influences that have carved the CNMI's unique identity. This examination aims to enrich our understanding of the CNMI's tourism landscape by closely examining its past, where the influences of Spanish, German, Japanese, and American powers intertwine to shape its cultural, governance, and economic fabric.

The CNMI's diverse and layered historical narrative, shaped by several global powers over centuries, uniquely contributed to its cultural identity, governance, economic systems, and, consequently, its approach to tourism. The CNMI's colonial past offering an insightful analysis of how different periods of rule have impacted the society and culture of the islands.

In the Spanish Colonial Era, geopolitical expansion and religious propagation objectives set the stage for a societal structure based on elitism and external control. The German Colonial Era, marked by a pragmatic economic focus, introduced new elites while further entrenching class divides. The Japanese period has brought another layer of transformation, with the islands becoming economic assets and experiencing infrastructural improvements, yet perpetuating the marginalization of indigenous populations. The American Colonial Era, which continues to the present, has reshaped the islands' governance and introduced new forms of elitism, significantly impacting their strategic and economic landscape.

These successive colonial periods have collectively shaped the CNMI's cultural identity, governance structures, and economic foundations. The legacy of colonialism is evident in the CNMI's contemporary society, where historical class structures and external influences continue to play a significant role. In the tourism industry, these legacies manifest in the ownership and management of tourism infrastructure, the types of tourism activities promoted, and the cultural narratives presented to visitors. The colonial past has also influenced the islands' reliance on external markets and investments for tourism development, continuing the dependency and external control pattern.

Exploring the CNMI through its historical narrative reveals patterns that align closely with the principles of Dependency Theory. This analytical approach is pivotal in understanding the dynamics between more affluent nations and regions like the CNMI, historically situated on the margins of the global economic system. Dependency Theory offers a nuanced perspective on the economic interdependencies and influences that have shaped the islands' development and continue to impact their societal and economic structure.

Dependency Theory emerged as a significant critique of conventional economic theories, particularly in the context of post-colonial nations. Pioneered by thinkers such as Andre Gunder Frank, Fernando Henrique Cardoso, and Theotonio Dos Santos, postulates that wealthier countries can make poorer nations dependent by integrating them into the world economy in a position of structural inferiority (Dietz, 1980). Essentially, 'core' countries exploit 'peripheral' countries for their resources and labor, leading to an outflow of wealth from the latter to the former (Dietz, 1980). This framework is crucial in understanding the economic trajectory and social changes in regions like the CNMI, which have navigated the post-colonial era and its complexities.

Central to Dependency Theory is the idea that 'core' countries, or those with advanced industrial economies, establish relationships that perpetuate the economic dependence of 'peripheral' countries. This dependence is maintained through various mechanisms, including trade practices, investment flows, and political influence. In these relationships, the 'core' countries often benefit from access to resources, labor, and markets in the 'peripheral' nations. At the same time, the latter remain in a subordinate position, with their economic structures often tailored to suit the needs of the more dominant countries.

Within the framework of the CNMI, Dependency Theory offers a perspective for examining the islands' economic growth and social evolution. The CNMI's history of colonial rule and subsequent economic interactions with more powerful nations reflects a classic case of dependency. The tourism industry, a significant economic pillar for the islands, can be seen through this lens. The dependency dynamics exemplify the industry's reliance on foreign investment, international tourists, and global market trends. This situation often results in most economic benefits flowing outwards to foreign entities, leaving the local economy and community with limited gains and heightened vulnerabilities to external fluctuations.

Moreover, the theory helps explain this dependency's social and cultural impacts. The CNMI's reliance on external influences has extended to cultural aspects, affecting everything from language use to cultural practices, as they often need to align with the preferences and expectations of tourists and foreign investors. Dependency

Theory thus offers a comprehensive framework for understanding the economic and social underpinnings of the CNMI's current state and its challenges in the tourism sector.

The tourism industry in the CNMI stands as the linchpin of its economic activities, drawing visitors worldwide with its picturesque landscapes and cultural richness. This industry influences not only the direct income from tourism ventures but also extends its impact to related areas like retail, dining, and broader entertainment sectors. The islands have invested significantly in developing tourism infrastructure, such as resorts, hotels, and various entertainment facilities, emphasizing tourism as a critical economic driver.

However, the heavy reliance on tourism comes with challenges, especially the dependency on factors beyond the CNMI's control. Global travel trends, economic conditions in crucial tourist-origin countries, and international political climates significantly shape the CNMI's tourism industry. Such dependence implies that negative shifts in these external factors could disproportionately affect the islands' economic health.

The CNMI's tourism sector also relies heavily on foreign investments and expertise. This reliance often results in a considerable portion of the economic gains flowing back to foreign stakeholders, reflecting the dependency dynamics where the local economy aligns itself to suit external interests. This situation highlights a core-periphery relationship, with the islands being the 'periphery' reliant on the 'core' for resources and investments, often at the cost of local economic retention.

This state of dependency presents various challenges, both economically and socially. From an economic standpoint, it restricts the diversification of the local economy and heightens vulnerability to global economic fluctuations. Socially, it leads to a workforce primarily engaged in the service sector, potentially neglecting other areas crucial for a balanced and robust economy.

The cultural aspect of this dependency is also significant. To appeal to tourist preferences, there is often a risk of local culture becoming commodified, which can dilute the authenticity of the CNMI's cultural heritage. Furthermore, prioritizing tourism can divert focus and resources from preserving and promoting local cultures and languages, impacting the islands' cultural identity.

Building upon understanding tourism's role as a form of economic dependency in the CNMI, we now focus on a specific aspect of this dynamic: the impact of foreign ownership and investment in the tourism sector. This shift is crucial as it unpacks how external economic influences shape the tourism industry's structure, affect the distribution of its profits, and contribute to broader economic inequalities within the islands.

In the CNMI's tourism sector, there has been a notable increase in foreign investment, which presents a mix of advantages and drawbacks. This external capital has been crucial in enhancing the islands' tourism facilities, elevating them to international standards, and positioning the CNMI on the global tourism map. Nevertheless, this trend also leads to a considerable portion of tourism-related income being channeled out of the CNMI rather than contributing to local reinvestment. Such a financial dynamic impacts the economic independence of the CNMI and poses questions about the viability and sustainability of depending extensively on foreign investment for long-term economic growth.

The distribution of tourism profits in the CNMI highlights a core-periphery dynamic, where the 'core'—in this case, foreign investors and corporations—extracts significant economic value, while the 'periphery'—the local economy and community—receives a smaller share of the benefits. This imbalance can lead to economic inequalities, with the wealth generated by the tourism industry not equitably benefiting the local population. The reliance on foreign investment also means that the CNMI's tourism sector is subject to external entities' priorities and market dynamics, which may not always align with the islands' interests or needs.

Moreover, the dominance of foreign entities in the CNMI's tourism sector can have ripple effects on the local economy. It can limit opportunities for local entrepreneurship in the tourism sector and restrict the development of locally-owned businesses. This situation can perpetuate economic disparities and hinder the growth of a diverse and resilient local economy.

While foreign investment is critical in the CNMI's tourism sector, it also brings economic equity and local empowerment challenges. The distribution of profits and the control exerted by foreign entities underscore the need for strategies that balance external investment with local interests and sustainable economic development. Understanding and addressing these issues is essential for ensuring the tourism sector drives economic growth and contributes to a fair and inclusive economic future for the CNMI.

Exploring tourism's socio-cultural impacts on the islands becomes equally important as we transition from examining the economic dimensions of foreign investment in the CNMI's tourism sector. This shift in focus from economic to cultural aspects is vital for understanding the comprehensive influence of tourism, not just as an economic activity but as a force that shapes culture, traditions, and identity.

Tourism in the CNMI has profoundly influenced the local culture, traditions, and languages. As the islands have increasingly catered to international visitors, there has been a notable shift in cultural practices, sometimes leading to the commercialization of local traditions. This commercialization often aims to make cultural practices more 'palatable' or 'attractive' to tourists, which can sometimes dilute their authenticity and meaning for the local community.

The impact of tourism is notably evident in the CNMI's culinary culture. The rich and distinct flavors, along with the unique preparation methods of traditional Chamorro and Carolinian dishes, are increasingly being altered or overshadowed by foods that cater more to the tastes of international tourists. These alterations in the culinary scene go beyond just changes in food; they affect the preservation of age-old recipes and methods. Furthermore, they also transform how the local community connects with and values its culinary traditions, potentially leading to a gradual detachment from their gastronomic roots.

Another area of impact is language use. As tourism becomes a dominant economic force, there is an increasing emphasis on languages favored by tourists, often leading to the marginalization of indigenous languages. This shift can have lasting implications on language preservation and the cultural identity of younger generations, who may grow up with less exposure to their native languages.

An example of a cultural shift due to tourism can be seen in local arts and performances. Traditional dances, music, and storytelling, integral parts of Chamorro and Carolinian cultures, are sometimes adapted to fit tourist expectations. This can result in greater visibility for these cultural forms and a version of culture that is more performance-oriented and less reflective of the true cultural essence.

The socio-cultural impacts of tourism in the CNMI are multifaceted, affecting everything from culinary traditions to language and the arts. While tourism can bring positive exposure to local culture, it also poses challenges in maintaining the authenticity and integrity of these cultural practices. Understanding and managing these impacts is crucial for ensuring that tourism development supports and celebrates the rich cultural heritage of the CNMI rather than diluting it.

Moving from the specific impacts on the cultural aspects to a broader issue that encompasses the entire spectrum of cultural expression in the CNMI: the challenge of cultural misrepresentation in tourism. This transition is crucial as it addresses how tourism marketing and practices can often distort or oversimplify local culture, prioritizing commercial appeal over authenticity.

Tourism marketing in the CNMI, like in many other destinations, sometimes falls into the trap of misrepresenting local culture to make it more appealing to a broader international audience. This can manifest in various forms, such as oversimplified or stereotyped portrayals of cultural practices, festivals, and daily life. Such representations may attract tourists but at the cost of presenting an inauthentic or incomplete picture of the CNMI's rich cultural tapestry.

The risks associated with this kind of cultural misrepresentation are significant. One primary concern is the potential erasure or homogenization of local culture. When the unique aspects of Chamorro and Carolinian cultures are diluted or adapted to fit a more generic or widely appealing narrative, there is a risk of losing the essence of these cultures. Over time, this can lead to a homogenization where distinct cultural practices and traditions lose their uniqueness and depth.

Another pressing concern is how these misrepresentations affect the local community's connection to their cultural roots. Inaccurate or shallow portrayals of their culture can create a rift between the community and its traditions, potentially weakening the sense of identity and pride, particularly among the youth. This disconnection poses a significant challenge in maintaining and passing cultural heritage to future generations.

To counter these challenges, promoting authentic cultural representation in tourism is essential. This involves a more collaborative approach to tourism marketing, where local communities are actively involved in how their culture is portrayed and shared with tourists. Efforts should be made to ensure that cultural presentations, whether in festivals, museum exhibits, or tourist activities, are developed with respect for cultural accuracy and integrity.

Furthermore, there is a need for educational initiatives aimed at tourists, helping them understand the depth and significance of the local culture beyond the superficial experiences. Such initiatives can foster a more respectful and meaningful interaction between tourists and the local culture. Addressing the challenges of cultural misrepresentation is crucial for sustainable tourism development in the CNMI. It requires a balanced approach that respects and celebrates the rich cultural heritage of the islands while also meeting the commercial objectives of the tourism industry.

In wrapping up the exploration of tourism's diverse impacts on the Commonwealth, it is essential to integrate the insights gathered throughout this chapter. The analysis has traversed the historical, economic, and socio-cultural terrain of the CNMI's tourism sector, revealing a complex interplay of factors from its colonial legacy to contemporary challenges. It is critical to address the remnants of colonialism and the ongoing economic dependencies that shape the

CNMI's tourism industry. A re-evaluation of tourism's development, marketing, and management is essential, aiming not just for economic gain but also for the respect and enhancement of local culture and the community. Recommendations for a sustainable future in the CNMI's tourism sector involve:

- encouraging active participation from local communities in decision-making processes
- ensuring authentic cultural representation in tourist experiences and
- diversifying the economy to mitigate dependency on external influences
- adopting sustainable practices to safeguard the islands' natural and cultural heritage for future generations.

The vision for the CNMI's tourism industry should focus on building a resilient, culturally respectful, and inclusive model. Such an approach promises to elevate the visitor experience and distribute the benefits of tourism more fairly among all community members.

Chapter 3

The Northern Mariana Islands: An Overlooked Paradise

The Northern Mariana Islands represent a gem concealed within the world map, discernible only by the most discerning eyes. Situated in the Western Pacific Ocean, the Northern Mariana Islands tend to be eclipsed by more famous island destinations such as Hawaii, the Caribbean, or the Maldives. This chapter aims to shift the perspective, moving beyond seeing these islands as small specks in the vast ocean and highlighting their unique and captivating beauty.

Located in the Western Pacific, the Northern Mariana Islands are fourteen distinct volcanic islands. Situated southeast of Japan, they form a natural frontier, with the Philippine Sea to their west and the immense Pacific Ocean to their east (Farrell, 1991). These islands are notably part of the Marianas Trench system, famous for containing the deepest parts of the world's oceans.

The landscape of each island in this chain is a testament to the dynamic forces of submarine volcanic activity. From rugged mountains that rise sharply against the sky to gentle hills and broad plateaus, the topography is as varied as it is dramatic. Despite their position in a tropical zone, the islands boast an array of microclimates. This diversity is due to their varying elevations and geographic placements. These islands have idyllic sandy beaches and vibrant coral reefs along the coasts, contrasting sharply with the wild, forested interiors marked by challenging terrains.

The individuality of each island in the Northern Mariana chain has been shaped by its seclusion, resulting in landscapes that are not unique but mesmerizing. These distinct natural features lend the islands an extraordinary charm, attracting those drawn to nature's rare and beautiful wonders.

On these islands, the seclusion has fostered a refuge teeming with diverse plant and animal species. The biodiversity is exceptional, with many species uniquely evolving in this region. The Northern Mariana Islands are a treasure trove of rare and distinctive flora and fauna, presenting a realm of exploration for both nature enthusiasts and scientific researchers, thanks to the array of species exclusive to this part of the globe.

The islands' flora are carpeted in lush forests teeming with native species. The ifit tree, the Intsia Bijuga, is particularly noteworthy (Vogt & Williams, 2004). This species is known for its durable hardwood and plays a crucial role in local ecosystems. The forests also abound with tangantangan shrubs, flame trees, and various species of orchids and ferns that brighten the understory. These plant species offer aesthetic appeal and create a lush habitat supporting many animal life.

As for fauna, the islands host a range of terrestrial and marine species that are as enchanting as they are diverse. Among the terrestrial mammals, the Mariana fruit bat holds a special place. Endemic to the region, this bat is considered a keystone species for pollination and seed dispersal (Fish and Wildlife Service, 2005). Birdwatchers would be delighted to spot the Mariana kingfisher, Mariana crow, and the endangered Nightingale reed-warbler, all native to the archipelago (Vogt & Williams, 2004). The Mariana Islands are also crucial in the East Asian-Australasian Flyway, serving as a vital stopover for various migrating bird species.

The marine environments surrounding the Northern Mariana Islands are equally stunning. The crystal-clear, turquoise waters and vibrant coral reefs bustling with life are home to a spectrum of fish, including clownfish, goatfish, butterflyfish, trumpetfish, lionfish, and many more. These waters are also a haven for sea turtles, such as the endangered green and hawksbill species regularly visiting these shores (Fisheries, 2023). Additionally, sharks, rays, and playful dolphins enhance the islands' reputation as a top-notch spot for observing marine wildlife in its natural habitat.

The coral reefs in the CNMI are among the world's most stunning. These ecosystems, encompassed by an intricate fringing and barrier reef system, provide a sanctuary for diverse marine life (Wusinich-Mendez & Trappe, 2007). However, these breathtaking reefs are at a crossroads, facing various challenges: climate change, coral bleaching, typhoons, and pollution pose significant threats (2007). These factors jeopardize the reefs' renowned beauty and critical role as a hub of marine biodiversity in the CNMI. Addressing these challenges within the CNMI is imperative, focusing on conservation strategies to ensure the survival and health of the marine life these reefs support, vital for the ecological balance of the local marine environment.

The Northern Mariana Islands' distinct geographic location has nurtured a haven for a wide variety of plant and animal life. Their remote positioning, the variety of microclimates, and diverse landscapes have fostered an environment where a rich and varied life thrives. From endemic hardwoods and vivid corals to endangered bird species and sea turtles, the natural world of these Pacific gems offers an unparalleled spectacle that captivates all who venture to explore it. The Northern Mariana Islands stand as a testament to the grandeur of nature when left undisturbed, a living, breathing museum of evolutionary wonder.

Just as the islands' unique ecology has drawn from a blend of different elements to thrive, its human history is a complex weave of traditions, beliefs, and narratives. Northern Mariana Islands' cultural tapestry is rich and diverse, deeply rooted in the traditions and histories of its indigenous inhabitants, the Chamorros, and the later arrivals, the Carolinians.

Before the archipelago was on global maps, the ancient Chamorro people had already claimed these islands as their home. It is believed that the Chamorros, following the wider Austronesian migratory path, settled in the Marianas around 1500 BC (Farrell, 1991). Their voyages from today's Southeast Asia regions showcased remarkable maritime prowess, using advanced celestial navigation techniques.

Settling down, the Chamorros soon fashioned a harmonious bond with the islands. They erected latte stone structures—tall megalithic pillars—that supported their homes and community centers (1991). Many of these latte stones remain today, standing as silent testaments to the architectural brilliance of the Chamorros.

In the Chamorro society, the social organization was centered around a matrilineal system, meaning lineage and inheritance were traced through the mother's side (2005). This society was distinctly hierarchical, with the three social classes, the matao class at the top, the acha'ot in the middle, and the manachang, the lowest class, primarily responsible for labor at the bottom (Tolentino, 2023). Such an arrangement facilitated equitable distribution of duties, fostered strong community bonds, and promoted efficient use of resources. Their livelihoods thrived on farming, fishing, and hunting. With the islands' fertile volcanic soil, they cultivated essential crops like taro, yams, and breadfruit.

Moreover, the Pacific's generous waters served a bounty of fish and other seafood integral to their diet. Chamorro also had a strong maritime tradition and an advanced outrigger canoe called proa. Proa was adeptly designed for speed and stability (2005). This vessel reflected the Chamorros' deep connection with the sea and their navigational expertise.

The Chamorros wove an intricate cultural tapestry filled with traditions, art, and spiritual beliefs as time unfolded. Respect for nature, ancestors, and spirits underpinned their worldview. Through storytelling, dances, and chants, they ensured the transmission of their lore and practices across generations.

While the Chamorros remain central to the history of the Northern Mariana Islands, another group, the Carolinians, has woven an equally intricate pattern into the islands' cultural fabric. The presence of the Carolinian community has significantly enriched the region's cultural diversity. This group, originating from the Caroline Islands in the central part of Micronesia, embarked on their journeys to the Marianas "in the early 19th century" (2023). Their arrival and settlement in the islands are a testament to the ongoing movement and exchange of cultures and peoples throughout the Pacific. Driven by various motivations—searching for more prosperous fishing grounds or the allure of new horizons—the Carolinians showcased remarkable navigational aptitude. Using nature's cues, like wave patterns and star paths, they made their way across vast oceanic distances. Upon their arrival in the Marianas, the relationship between the Carolinians and the Chamorros, initially marked by the hesitations of newcomers meeting established residents, gradually transformed into mutual respect and cooperation. As interactions deepened, so did the merging of cultures through intermarriages, trade, and shared rituals.

The Carolinians contributed their distinct cultural elements to the Marianas. They introduced their versions of music, dance, and oral traditions, which, over time, found a harmonious place beside the Chamorro practices. Vibrant Carolinian dances and melodies have become a staple in many islands' communal celebrations. One of the most notable Carolinian traditions is their unique matrilineal clan system. This system aligns with the Chamorro matrilineal heritage and further reinforces the importance of women and familial ties in determining societal roles and lineage. Additionally, the Carolinian community brought an array of crafts and techniques, from intricate weaving patterns for mats and garments to specialized fishing methods that capitalized on their deep understanding of the ocean.

Today, the combined influence of Chamorro and Carolinian cultures is palpable throughout the Northern Mariana Islands. Their languages, traditions, and communal practices coalesce, creating a vibrant cultural mosaic. They exemplify resilience, adaptation, and unity, reflecting a shared reverence for the islands they have shaped and cherished.

The Northern Mariana Islands, often overlooked in the global spotlight, are a magnificent repository of natural wonders and cultural heritage. Rooted in the Chamorro and Carolinian peoples' deep histories and vibrant traditions, the islands represent a compelling narrative of human resilience, ingenuity, and a symbiotic relationship with the environment. From ancient latte stone structures to evocative dances and music, each aspect of the islands bears witness to its rich past and dynamic present. The diverse ecosystems, teeming with species unique to these shores, add another layer of importance to this Pacific archipelago. While they may stand in the shadow of more famous destinations, the true allure of the Northern Mariana Islands is their extraordinary convergence of natural beauty and cultural richness, making them a destination worthy of deeper exploration for any traveler.

Chapter 4

Establishment of Tourism in the CNMI

The Commonwealth of the Northern Mariana Islands stands as a testament to the intricate dance between ambition and reality in the realm of tourism. As the islands sought to establish themselves as a premier destination, they grappled with the dual influences of elitism and third-world paradigms, each shaping their trajectory in unique ways.

Rewind to the 1970s, a time of significant global political shifts. For the CNMI, it was the dawning of a transformative phase. Prior to this era, the islands existed under the Trust Territory status, a relatively inconspicuous designation. However, the onset of the 1970s brought with it the promise of change. The CNMI embarked on its journey to become a self-governing commonwealth under the United States (CNMI, 2023). This transition was more than just symbolic; it bore tangible benefits and strategic implications.

For the CNMI, this newfound status came with specific rights and liberties. In particular, the archipelago was granted the authority to determine its wage policies and immigration rules. The bold decision to set a minimum wage below the U.S. standard in the CNMI was a clear demonstration of its independence. While this may initially seem like a step backward, within the specific context of the CNMI, it was actually a calculated strategy. This move underscored the CNMI's ambition to become a more appealing location for investment.

One cannot stress enough the significance of the CNMI's geographic positioning. Tucked away in close proximity to Asian economic giants such as Japan, Korea, and China, the islands were geographically poised to serve as an exotic escape for Asia's burgeoning middle class and elite. This proximity was about more than just reducing travel time. It symbolized the CNMI's potential role as a bridge between the East and the West—a luxurious midpoint that was both familiar and foreign.

However, like all pursuits of greatness, the CNMI's journey was challenging. The dream of transforming into a top-tier tourist destination highlighted the shortcomings in the archipelago's infrastructure. It became increasingly clear that, in their present state, the islands were not prepared to accommodate a large number of international visitors.

Accommodation was the first primary concern. The CNMI had lodgings, but they were far from what international tourists, especially those from affluent backgrounds, would expect. The islands needed accommodations that ranged from budget-friendly options to luxurious resorts.

The CNMI's roads, which had served the local population adequately until then, were also put to the test. With the expected surge in tourist vehicles, it was clear that the current road networks would be insufficient. Expansions, upgrades, and maintenance became the need of the hour.

Next was the human resource challenge. The local populace was enthusiastic about the islands' tourism aspirations, but there was a palpable skills gap. Key roles, ranging from hotel management to culinary expertise, were lacking in trained professionals. It was clear that either the CNMI had to invest in training its citizens or open its doors to skilled workers from abroad.

Finally, the dream of elevating the CNMI to a top-tier tourist destination came with a hefty price tag. High-end resorts, modern transportation facilities, and international standard amenities—all of these required considerable capital. Given its nascent stage in the global tourism scene, the CNMI faced the daunting task of attracting domestic and international investments.

Despite the looming challenges, the 1980s and 1990s were decades of proactive action for the CNMI. Recognizing the need for a centralized body to spearhead tourism growth, the Marianas Visitors Bureau was established in 1976. This was not just another bureaucratic organization; it was the CNMI's flagship institution tasked with the critical role of marketing and nurturing the islands' emerging tourism sector.

Backed by the U.S. Federal Government and buoyed by private investments, the CNMI underwent infrastructural metamorphosis during these two decades. One could witness the transformation almost in real-time. The Saipan International Airport, previously modest in its operations, expanded its reach, inviting international airlines and charter flights. Luxury resorts, previously a rarity, began mushrooming across the islands. Roads were widened, modernized, and beautified. Utility systems, a crucial yet often overlooked aspect, were upgraded to handle the anticipated demands of a bustling tourist hub.

However, the most pivotal moment arrived when the CNMI established direct flight connections with major Asian cities in the 1980s. This move was not merely logistical; it was symbolic. The CNMI, with its proximity to the Asian continent and its unique distinction as a U.S. territory, sent out a powerful message of accessibility.

Nevertheless, with growth came a new set of challenges. As the CNMI threw open its doors to international tourists, a cultural conundrum arose. The islands were at a juncture, torn between showcasing their rich Chamorro and Carolinian heritage and molding themselves to the tastes and preferences of their international visitors.

In the years that followed, the CNMI's tourism strategy, perhaps swayed by the success of other Pacific destinations, leaned towards the familiar. The islands began echoing Hawaiian vibes, replicating Hawaiian cultural performances, and marketed the CNMI as a "mini Hawaii".

This era also saw the islands grappling with socio-economic complexities. The burgeoning tourism sector led to an increased demand for labor. To meet this, the CNMI began to rely on foreign workers, predominantly from Southeast Asia and other Pacific regions. While aiding the economy, this influx also brought with it concerns related to wage disparities, social integration, and labor rights.

In essence, the establishment of tourism in the CNMI is a tale of victories and obstacles. The calculated planning and execution resulted in a booming industry that revolutionized the islands' economic landscape. Nevertheless, it highlighted stark disparities and serious sociocultural issues that continue to influence the CNMI's tourism industry's path. The following chapters will delve deeper into these challenges and the steps taken to address them, providing a thorough understanding of the CNMI's complex and dynamic tourism industry.

Chapter 5

Influence of the Island's Elite on the Tourism Industry

In the dynamic landscape of the Northern Mariana Islands' tourism industry, the role played by the local elite stands out as both influential and transformative. This chapter delves into the significant impact these key figures have had in shaping the direction, character, and growth of the tourism sector in the islands. The impact of these individuals and organizations is multifaceted and extensive, shaping everything from policy choices to how cultures are represented.

In the Northern Mariana Islands, 'elite' describes a specific set of individuals and organizations that hold significant sway over the area's social and economic landscape. This group typically includes political leaders, established business magnates, influential landowners, and other personalities with significant societal sway. Their influence stems from various sources, including wealth, control over critical resources, political leverage, and social standing.

Understanding the role of these elites is crucial in comprehending the broader picture of the tourism industry in the Northern Mariana Islands. Their decisions, investments, and policies have shaped the physical landscape of tourism and influenced the islands' cultural and economic fabric. This chapter explores the depth and breadth of the elite's involvement in the tourism industry, examining the positive developments and challenges arising from their dominance.

The elite class in the Northern Mariana Islands, pivotal in shaping the tourism industry, comprises a diverse and influential group. This includes political leaders directly impacting tourism-related policies and development strategies through their significant governmental positions. Business tycoons, owning and controlling major tourism enterprises, also form a part of this elite class. Their investments in resorts, hotels, and other facilities are central to tourism. Another crucial segment comprises powerful landowners, who, holding vast tracts of land, influence the development and direction of tourism infrastructure. Additionally, influential societal figures – cultural icons, celebrities, or high-profile personalities – shape public opinion and trends within the tourism sector.

The power and influence of these elites stem from various sources. Business tycoons and landowners wield economic control and wealth, enabling them to drive investments and decisions in the tourism sector. Political leaders exert their influence through policy-making and legislative actions, which can facilitate or hinder tourism development. With their control over a critical resource, landowners directly impact the type and scale of tourism activities. Influential societal figures, through their status and public reach, can shape cultural perceptions and trends in tourism, both locally and internationally. Additionally, the networks and connections between these groups allow for a synergistic approach, further amplifying their collective influence on the tourism industry in the Northern Mariana Islands. Understanding the interplay of these diverse power sources is essential in comprehending the dynamics and evolution of tourism in the region.

In the Northern Mariana Islands, the elite's ownership and investment in tourism facilities are critical in shaping the direction of the tourism sector. This influential group holds significant stakes in major establishments such as hotels and resorts, a factor that profoundly affects the tourism landscape. The luxurious hotels and resorts, often under the control of this elite class, set the benchmark for service quality and guest experiences in the region. Their dominance in the hospitality sector reflects not only their economic interests but also their strategic influence over the tourism market.

The investment choices of these elite figures and groups are pivotal in determining the direction of the tourism industry. When they channel funds into new developments, like upscale resorts, entertainment venues, or infrastructural enhancements, they effectively dictate the nature and character of tourism in the islands. These investments are driven by business insight, profit motives, and strategic planning, aligning with broader economic objectives like attracting tourists and catering to particular market segments.

However, the impact of these investments extends beyond mere economic implications. The type of tourism fostered by these developments – luxury-focused or geared towards mass appeal – significantly influences various aspects of island life. This includes employment patterns, socio-economic conditions, and even the cultural landscape. The tourism facilities developed and managed by the elite are often central to attracting visitors, thereby playing a crucial role in driving the local tourism economy.

In essence, the involvement of the elite in the tourism facilities of the Northern Mariana Islands is a dynamic and influential factor. Their capacity to invest in, develop, and upgrade these facilities in response to market trends, technological advancements, and consumer preferences is crucial for maintaining the islands' competitive edge in tourism. The ownership and investment decisions of the elite not only shape the physical infrastructure of tourism but also define the quality and appeal of the CNMI as a tourist destination, making an understanding of these dynamics essential for grasping the broader picture of the region's tourism sector.

In the Northern Mariana Islands, the intersection of the elite's influence with political decision-making significantly impacts the formulation and implementation of tourism policies. Members of the elite class, who often possess or are closely linked with political power, play a crucial role in shaping the tourism sector's legislative and regulatory framework.

Through their political connections, these elite members can influence various tourism-related policies. This includes decisions on zoning regulations, environmental standards, tax incentives for tourism investments, and even the marketing strategies employed to promote the islands. Their involvement can steer policies in directions that primarily benefit their interests, often focusing on maximizing profits and expanding their tourism ventures.

However, the implications of these policies extend far beyond the boardrooms and political offices. They profoundly impact the islands' social, economic, and environmental landscapes. For instance, policies favoring large-scale tourism developments can significantly change land use, affecting local communities and the natural environment. While such developments might boost the economy through increased tourist arrivals and job creation, they can also strain local resources, disrupt traditional ways of life, and lead to environmental degradation.

Furthermore, the concentration of policy influence in the hands of a few elite members raises concerns about equitable development and representation. Decisions that prioritize elite interests might overlook the broader needs and voices of the local population. This situation can take different forms, ranging from restricted community involvement in decision-making to inadequate attention to the islands' and their residents' long-term well-being.

The participation of influential individuals with political connections in formulating tourism policies in the Northern Mariana Islands presents a complex scenario. On the one hand, it can spur quick progress and economic expansion in tourism. On the other, it raises concerns about maintaining this growth in a sustainable, fair manner that benefits the islands and their communities. Understanding the nuances of this policy influence and its widespread implications is vital to assessing the region's current and future direction of tourism.

In the Northern Mariana Islands, the elite class's control and allocation of land significantly influence the development and direction of the tourism industry. Given the limited availability and high value of land in the islands, the decisions made by these powerful landowners can have far-reaching implications for the nature and scope of tourism development.

The elite, often owning extensive tracts of land, can decide how this land is utilized. Their choices often favor large-scale tourism projects such as expansive resorts, golf courses, and other major attractions. These developments, while potentially lucrative and instrumental in drawing a significant number of tourists, can profoundly alter the landscape and character of the islands. The construction and operation of such extensive facilities often require substantial resources and can lead to environmental challenges, such as habitat disruption, increased waste, and water resource depletion.

Moreover, these large-scale projects can create tension with more sustainable, community-focused initiatives. The preference for grand tourism ventures can overshadow smaller, local, and eco-friendly projects that may be more sustainable and beneficial to the local communities. These smaller initiatives often focus on preserving the islands' natural environment and cultural heritage, fostering responsible tourism that economically and socially benefits local inhabitants.

The dominance of the elite in land control and allocation decisions can thus skew the development of tourism towards their interests, sometimes at the expense of broader community needs and environmental sustainability. This raises important questions about balancing profit-driven tourism development and preserving the islands' natural and cultural assets. The primary challenge is to find equilibrium where tourism thrives without undermining the local environment's health and the community's overall welfare.

The control exerted by the elite over land in the Northern Mariana Islands is crucial in determining the direction of tourism development. The preference for large-scale projects often results in a tension between the pursuit of economic gains and the need for sustainable, community-oriented tourism practices. Understanding and addressing this dynamic is crucial for ensuring that tourism development in the islands is balanced, responsible, and beneficial for all stakeholders involved.

In the Northern Mariana Islands, the elite class not only exerts influence over tourism's economic and policy aspects but also plays a significant role in the cultural domain. As custodians of the islands' heritage, their influence extends to how the local culture is presented and promoted to tourists. This involvement profoundly impacts the narrative surrounding the islands' cultural offerings and how tourists experience the local heritage.

By virtue of their resources and social standing, the elite often find themselves in positions where they can shape the cultural experiences offered to tourists. This includes deciding which aspects of the local culture to highlight in tourism marketing, how to present cultural events and festivals, and how local history and traditions are interpreted and showcased. Their decisions can significantly influence tourists' perceptions of the islands' cultural identity.

However, the elite's role in cultural promotion is complex. While their resources and influence can help preserve and showcase the islands' cultural heritage, there is also a risk of commercializing and commodifying culture in a way that may not authentically represent the local communities. Promoting certain cultural aspects over others, often guided by market trends and profitability, can lead to a skewed representation of the islands' rich heritage.

Moreover, the elite's control over cultural narratives can sometimes overshadow grassroots cultural movements and the voices of local artists and cultural practitioners. This can result in a homogenized and possibly inauthentic cultural experience for tourists that caters to popular perceptions and stereotypes rather than the essence of the islands' cultural diversity.

The elite's influence in cultural promotion and custodianship in the Northern Mariana Islands is critical in shaping how the islands' heritage is projected to the outside world. Their decisions and actions in this domain have the power to either enrich or dilute the cultural experience for tourists. A balanced approach that respects and authentically represents the local culture while tapping into its tourism potential is essential for preserving the islands' cultural integrity and ensuring a genuine cultural exchange between the local community and visitors.

The elite-driven model of tourism in the Northern Mariana Islands has been criticized, particularly regarding its effects on inequality, the marginalization of local communities, and its environmental and societal impacts. One of the primary criticisms is the concentration of tourism benefits within the elite class, leading to a disparity where a select few enjoy the majority of economic gains. This approach exacerbates existing social inequalities and often results in the broader local community being sidelined regarding economic opportunities and participation in decision-making processes.

In addition to economic concerns, there are cultural implications. The elite's control over cultural representation in tourism can lead to modifying the local heritage, where cultural elements are altered or overshadowed to cater to commercial interests. This can dilute the authenticity of the islands' cultural identity and traditions.

Environmental concerns are also prominent in critiques of elite-driven tourism. Major tourism initiatives, often supported by influential figures, pose a significant risk of environmental damage, such as habitat destruction, heightened pollution, and resource exhaustion. The ecological effects of these projects are a pressing concern, with the possibility of enduring impacts on the sustainability and vitality of the islands' natural ecosystems and resources.

Furthermore, the societal impact of this tourism development model can be profound. It often leads to increased living costs and the possibility of local communities being uprooted due to the construction of tourism facilities. Additionally, there is a danger of cultural erosion, with the commercial demands of tourism potentially overshadowing and diminishing the traditional ways of life and values cherished by the local community.

The elite-driven model has indeed fueled the expansion of the Northern Mariana Islands' tourism sector but has also led to notable challenges. These issues cover a range of problems, such as economic disparities, the commercial exploitation of cultural aspects, environmental degradation, and social disruption. Tackling these matters is vital to creating a tourism approach that is more equitable and sustainable, benefiting the broader community while safeguarding the islands' natural and cultural heritage.

The emphasis by the elite on immediate financial gains in the Northern Mariana Islands tourism sector brings into question the industry's long-term health and sustainability. This approach, often prioritizing immediate financial returns, tends to overlook the broader environmental and socio-cultural impacts, potentially compromising the future health and attractiveness of the tourism sector. The challenge lies in balancing the quest for rapid economic gains with preserving the islands' unique natural and cultural assets, ensuring the tourism industry remains sustainable for future generations.

The influence of the elite on the tourism industry's growth in the Northern Mariana Islands has been significant. Nevertheless, this impact has resulted in prominent problems such as economic inequality, the commodification of culture, environmental harm, and social unrest. These challenges call for a thorough reevaluation of the elite's involvement in the tourism industry and underscore the need for adopting more equitable and sustainable development approaches. It is crucial to implement strategies that equally value economic advancement, social fairness, and the protection of the environment.

Efforts to mitigate the negative impacts of elite-driven tourism and promote equitable growth could include community-based tourism initiatives, stringent environmental regulations for tourism projects, and platforms for local communities to participate in tourism planning. Additionally, promoting authentic cultural experiences in tourism can help preserve the islands' heritage while offering unique experiences to visitors. Ultimately, steering the tourism development towards an inclusive and sustainable model is crucial, ensuring that it remains a source of prosperity and pride for the entire community while preserving the rich cultural and natural legacy of the islands.

Chapter 6

Impact of Third-World Frameworks on Tourism Development

In the dynamic world of global tourism, specific trends and influences shape the narratives and destinies of destinations, especially those nestled in the Pacific region. The CNMI stands at a unique crossroads, influenced by its historical legacy and the forces of modern economic paradigms. As we delve deeper into this chapter, we focus on the profound impact of Third-World frameworks on CNMI's tourism development.

"Third-world frameworks" often bring notions of underdevelopment, colonial residues, and economic chains that bind nations to specific trajectories. While these connotations hold weight, the intricate relationship between such frameworks and tourism is complex. Tourism, seen as a golden goose for many developing regions, holds a duality: it can be a path to progress or a cycle of continued dependency.

For the Northern Mariana Islands, where history's echoes are palpable in every corner, it is essential to grasp how these Third-World frameworks have molded its tourism sector. Our exploration will take us from the remnants of colonial footprints to the modern corridors of global business, from the aspirations of islanders to the blueprints of international stakeholders.

As we navigate this journey, we aim to understand the nuances and intricacies of how these frameworks have steered CNMI's tourism, paving the way for deeper discussions on sustainability and empowerment in the chapters ahead.

Navigating the intricate pathways of global economic and socio-political narratives, we are consistently drawn to the foundational principles that define Third-World frameworks. These fundamental principles, shaped by significant historical events, played an essential role in the fates of many countries. The CNMI in the Pacific is a prominent example of this.

During the late 15th and early 16th centuries, a significant era of exploration unfolded, marked by the pursuit of European powers to discover and annex new territories. However, this fervor for discovery soon transformed into an era of exploitation, where newfound regions became mere assets in the grand game of imperial dominance.

Emerging from the shadows of Cold War geopolitics, the term 'Third World' initially offered a classification for nations outside the immediate influence of NATO and Communist blocs (Britanica, 2023). Nevertheless, as global dynamics evolved, this term began to encompass nations struggling with the challenges of underdevelopment and remnants of colonial subjugation, underscoring the stark disparities and power imbalances inherent in the global order.

While the chains of a direct colonial rule might have been discarded, the specter of neocolonialism loomed large. This more insidious form of control, often manifesting economically and politically rather than territorially, perpetuated the inequalities of yesteryears. Instruments of this new dominance included international institutions, trade agreements, and the ever-growing influence of multinational corporations.

Many nations viewed tourism as a beacon of hope in their quest for economic revival post-independence. The unique allure of natural landscapes, rich cultures, and historical landmarks presented an enticing proposition for Third-World nations. However, this outward push towards tourism, frequently driven by external forces, was fraught with pitfalls. The experiences of the CNMI, mirror the challenges faced by many such nations, ranging from economic over-dependency to the gradual dilution of cultural essence.

The latter part of the 20th century, characterized by accelerated globalization, witnessed a dynamic interplay of cultures, economies, and political ideologies (Annan, 1999). This era of interconnectedness, while bringing forth myriad growth opportunities, also exposed Third-World nations to the whims and volatilities of global markets. Herein, multinational corporations began to play an outsized role, often overshadowing local interests and sometimes imposing terms that were misaligned with the best interests of these nations.

Grasping this rich sequence of events and influences equips us with the perspective needed to understand the Northern Mariana Islands' unique journey. The story, resonating with the experiences of many Third-World nations, showcases the interplay of challenges and opportunities arising from historical imprints and modern economic constructs.

In the global economic landscape, tourism presents a unique opportunity for nations, especially those looking for rapid growth and development. This opportunity is particularly enticing for Third-World countries, offering the potential for a steady flow of foreign currency, job creation, and a platform to share their cultural and natural assets with the world.

For many Third-World regions, the emergence of tourism is often more of a response to external interests than an internally driven initiative. Driven by the potential for immediate economic benefits, these areas readily open their natural wonders, historical sites, and cultural experiences to visitors. This welcoming approach often focuses on infrastructure development, such as hotels and transportation systems, to cater to the expected increase in tourists. However, critical aspects like sustainability, cultural integrity, and genuine community involvement might take a back seat in this rush.

Building a robust tourism sector requires significant capital, often more than available within these nations. This financial gap becomes an attractive prospect for foreign investments. Multinational corporations step in to fill this void with their vast resources and expertise. They promise advanced resorts, efficient operational systems, and marketing efforts that can position a destination prominently on the global tourism map. However, their involvement comes with challenges. While they can elevate a region's tourism profile, they might also direct a substantial portion of the revenue away from the local community. Their global-centric strategies might not always align with local values and priorities, leading to potential friction.

As external players enter the scene, there is a noticeable alteration in the balance of influence. Local communities and administrations harboring growth ambitions often find themselves in the shadow of these formidable corporations. These foreign entities frequently steered the decision-making processes, ideally a realm for local stakeholders' collective voice. They dictate the terms, from land allocation to operational procedures, occasionally sidelining the genuine needs and aspirations of the locals. Such a dynamic evokes memories of past colonial times, where a region's assets were primarily harnessed for the advantage of outsiders, leaving the indigenous community navigating the aftermath.

Observing the Northern Mariana Islands, one can see that these worldwide trends are also evident here. With their plentiful natural wonders and rich cultural heritage, these islands are an ideal spot for tourists. However, the critical challenge is ensuring that tourism growth is a joint endeavor involving substantial input from the local community and fair distribution of its advantages.

The CNMI's tourism sector has been shaped significantly by foreign investments. As investors recognized the potential returns from the islands' tourism, capital steadily flowed into the region. These investments, often under the banner of multinational corporations, drove the development of infrastructure, services, and the overall tourism ethos of the CNMI. Resorts emerged, transportation systems evolved, and the islands started gaining prominence in international travel narratives.

Land rights have been a significant focal point in the relationship between the CNMI and foreign investors. Article XII of the CNMI Constitution safeguards the land ownership rights of the local population, ensuring that freehold remains exclusive to the indigenous community (Cabrera, 2021). While this provision protects the land ownership rights of the local people, it does not preclude them from leasing their property. As a result, many investors have sought to lease either public lands or properties from private citizens for tourism-related developments. However, to navigate the restrictions of Article XII, some investors have resorted to indirect strategies. They often collaborate with local individuals, persuading them to purchase land on their behalf, effectively bypassing the legal constraints. While circumventing the spirit of the law, this approach has led to tensions and conflicts over land usage and the actual beneficiaries of these arrangements. Meanwhile, the government has the discretion to lease public lands, which often becomes another avenue for investors to pursue their interests.

Further complicating the landscape was the issue of local participation in the burgeoning tourism sector. While the influx of investment promised job opportunities, the reality often diverged from expectations. Many managerial and decision-making roles in the tourism establishments were occupied by individuals outside the CNMI, relegating locals to roles with limited upward mobility. This impacted the economic distribution and influenced how the local culture was represented and marketed to tourists.

The islands' heavy reliance on tourism also introduced economic vulnerabilities. As tourism became a dominant economic pillar, the CNMI's financial health became tethered to the unpredictable ebb and flow of global travel trends. Moreover, since many significant tourism establishments were under foreign ownership, a substantial chunk of the generated revenue would leave the islands, constraining the economic benefits for the indigenous community.

Facing these multifaceted challenges, the CNMI is at a pivotal juncture. While tourism offers avenues for economic growth, it also presents complexities that warrant thoughtful navigation. A balanced approach, honoring foreign investment interests and the indigenous community's rights, is paramount to ensuring a sustainable and inclusive future for the islands' tourism sector. To further contextualize the CNMI's position, a comparative lens with other Pacific island nations or territories can provide valuable insights.

With its myriad islands and unique cultures, the Pacific region has long been a canvas where global powers painted their narratives. Often presented as an economic savior, tourism has played a significant role in these tales. Drawing comparisons with other Pacific island nations or territories and their experiences with third-world tourism models is beneficial to understanding the CNMI's position within this larger picture.

CNMI and Vanuatu:

With its vibrant Melanesian heritage, Vanuatu has seamlessly integrated cultural events and traditions into its tourism sector (2023). Similarly, the CNMI, graced by its Chamorro and Carolinian backgrounds, is at a pivotal point where its indigenous practices can be the centerpiece of its tourism strategy. On the land front, while Vanuatu leans heavily on customary ownership (Lindstrom), the CNMI has constitutional provisions safeguarding indigenous land rights. Both regions aim to provide visitors with an authentic cultural immersion shaped by their unique land ownership systems.

CNMI and Samoa:

Samoa's deep-rooted Polynesian identity manifests in its tourism approach, offering a harmonious model where culture and tourism exist (Twining-Ward, 2002). The CNMI can extract valuable lessons from Samoa's methodology, embedding indigenous tales, art forms, and traditions into its burgeoning tourism sector. These regions symbolize the potential of crafting genuine and memorable experiences by intertwining land, culture, and tourism.

CNMI and Tonga:

Tonga's tourism, enriched by its regal ceremonies and traditions, carves a distinct space in the Pacific's tourism landscape (The Adept Traveler, 2023). The CNMI, with its cultural richness, can frame a tourism narrative that accentuates its indigenous voices and practices. Their approach to land, emphasizing the preservation of indigenous rights while promoting tourism, showcases a balance between cultural integrity and economic aspirations.

CNMI and Kiribati:

Kiribati's allegiance to its Micronesian roots, mirrored in its tourism endeavors (PATA, 2023), stands as an exemplar for the CNMI. By championing indigenous traditions, from music to dance to narratives, the CNMI can curate a standout tourism experience. Both territories can prioritize sustainable land use and foster a tourism environment that respects and preserves their natural splendor.

CNMI and Guam:

In close quarters and sharing historical ties with the CNMI, Guam boasts a well-evolved tourism industry. While U.S. policies have influenced both, their cultural narratives exhibit variations. Guam's seasoned tourism sector provides insights into the intricacies of upholding Chamorro traditions amidst commercial demands. The CNMI can derive wisdom from Guam's trajectory, identifying potential challenges and opportunities in synergizing culture, land use, and tourism.

In gleaning insights from these comparisons, a recurrent aspiration emerges across the Pacific territories: the quest to weave a tourism narrative that harmoniously marries culture, land, and economic pursuits. Drawing comparisons with other Pacific Island nations or territories and their experiences with third-world tourism models offers valuable insights into the CNMI's position within this broader landscape. Building on these comparative insights, we must delve deeper into the potential consequences that third-world tourism frameworks could impose on the CNMI.

Tourism, with its promise of economic growth, often masks the complex outcomes associated with adopting third-world frameworks, a reality deeply felt in the CNMI. This archipelago, steeped in a rich tapestry of history, culture, and untouched beauty, confronts the diverse challenges presented by this tourism model.

While tourism brings in a surge of foreign revenue, its dispersion across the local economy can be lopsided. Small local enterprises may struggle against the might of global corporations, feeling the pinch of competition. Moreover, while the tourism sector might offer many job opportunities, many of these roles could be confined to low-paying segments. The island's heavy reliance on tourism also exposes its economy to the whims of global trends, including economic shifts or sudden events that disrupt travel.

The environmental implications are equally concerning. The CNMI's captivating natural landscapes, a major tourist draw, face potential degradation. Excessive tourism might strain the islands' beaches, coral ecosystems, and other natural wonders. The influx of tourists often correlates with heightened waste, particularly of the non-recyclable variety, presenting significant environmental dilemmas. Moreover, if not executed carefully, hasty infrastructural development can disrupt the natural habitats, affecting the area's ecological harmony.

The potential dilution of the CNMI's cultural essence is a subtler but deeply significant consequence. The islands' vibrant Chamorro and Carolinian legacies are under the specter of commodification. There is a risk that time-honored dances, ceremonies, tales, and even languages could be altered to meet tourist demands, compromising their authenticity. Similarly, the islands' distinct culinary arts might be overshadowed as global culinary trends take precedence.

As the CNMI charts its course, it is faced with a twofold task: harnessing the economic boons of tourism while steadfastly safeguarding its unparalleled socio-cultural and environmental treasures. The trajectory of the CNMI's tourism industry rests on achieving this equilibrium, aspiring for an economically thriving future and true to its roots. To appreciate the depth of this challenge and the nuances involved, examining specific projects and initiatives that have influenced the islands provides a clearer perspective.

In the CNMI's pursuit of tourism-led growth, there have been projects and initiatives that, while promising prosperity, have inadvertently eroded the islands' unique character. The allure of economic dividends sometimes overshadowed the need to preserve the CNMI's essence. Delving deeper into these undertakings unveils a series of compromises and losses that have put the islands' distinct identity at risk.

Saipan's Upscale Resort Expansion:

Saipan's push towards luxury resorts, predominantly backed by foreign investment, aimed to establish the island as a coveted destination for high-end travelers. These ventures also redefined Saipan's cultural and physical ambiance by creating job opportunities and drawing tourists. A significant portion of the revenue earned went to parent companies abroad. These resorts, tailored for an international clientele, often marginalized local traditions and tastes, resulting in a potential cultural dilution.

The Diminishing Visibility of Chamorro and Carolinian Cultures:

With tourism endeavors striving to cater to global audiences, the intrinsic Chamorro and Carolinian cultures frequently got sidelined. Rather than being a focal point, these age-old traditions were sometimes limited to sporadic events or periodic celebrations.

The lack of consistent platforms to exhibit and honor these cultures implies that numerous tourists depart from CNMI with a shallow grasp of its cultural richness. This misrepresents the islands' authentic identity and stirs apprehensions about younger generations drifting away from their cultural foundations.

Diving's Dual Edge:

The marine wonders of CNMI, especially its diving spots, have attracted numerous enthusiasts. However, the increasing footfall at these sites began exerting pressure on marine habitats. The pristine allure of coral reefs, a primary draw for many, began witnessing degradation, attributable to factors like intensive diving and pollution. Although diving brought economic benefits, it also posed environmental concerns that cast doubt over its long-term viability.

Environmental Concerns with Infrastructure Development:

The accelerated infrastructural advancements to cater to the swelling tourist numbers often came with ecological implications. Projects, if not judiciously designed, risked disturbing the indigenous ecosystems. In the haste of progress, these ventures' enduring sustainability and ecological ramifications were sometimes overlooked.

The case studies elucidate that while bringing economic prospects to CNMI, the third-world tourism paradigms concurrently ushered in challenges, especially regarding cultural authenticity and ecological conservation. The islands now face the imperative task of amplifying the Chamorro and Carolinian narratives and ensuring their dominant presence in the tourism discourse. At this juncture, CNMI's choices will determine if its tourism blueprint respects its legacy while seeking progress.

Drawing from these insights and the intricate dance between opportunities and challenges, it is essential to consider the wider consequences and outline a strategy for moving ahead. As we transition into concluding thoughts for this chapter, we must synthesize the lessons learned and contemplate the future trajectory for CNMI's tourism industry.

With their intricate blend of history, culture, and untouched nature, the Northern Mariana Islands stand at a pivotal intersection of historical influences and future ambitions. Delving into the CNMI's experiences within third-world tourism frameworks has provided a multifaceted perspective rife with promise and caution.

While the allure of tourism has undeniably boosted the islands' economy, it is essential to recognize and address the visible and hidden costs. A recurring motif throughout this chapter has been the quest for equilibrium between economic aspirations and preserving the essence of the CNMI. The various case studies discussed shed light on the intricate challenges that regions, bearing the imprints of colonial pasts, face when navigating the intricate terrain of global tourism.

Ensuring the enduring prominence of the Chamorro and Carolinian heritages is crucial. The risk of these rich traditions being overshadowed in the tourism narrative underscores the existing imbalances and the dangers of neglecting native perspectives. Additionally, the environmental concerns emphasize the pressing need for a development approach that safeguards the islands' natural treasures, ensuring they remain for generations.

Looking forward, the CNMI stands on the brink of defining its future. The insights from its past and ongoing engagements with third-world tourism paradigms will be instrumental. The islands have a golden chance, and arguably an obligation, to craft a tourism story that champions economic ambitions but remains rooted in cultural authenticity and environmental responsibility.

Chapter 7

There is No Balance Between Third World Frameworks and Sustainable Tourism

Balancing Third World frameworks with sustainable tourism often presents itself as a tantalizing mirage, especially in regions like the CNMI. Beneath the allure of this paradise, with its azure waters and verdant landscapes, lies a tumultuous reality. The islands, for all their innate beauty and culture, are ensnared in an intricate web of socio-economic constraints and external dependencies. In global tourism, where destinations often grapple with striking the right balance between development and preservation, the CNMI confronts a particularly daunting paradox. The structures it operates within, characterized by immediate economic pursuits and reliance on external forces, starkly clash with the tenets of sustainability. This chapter delves into this dissonance, shedding light on the seemingly insurmountable chasm between the CNMI's existing frameworks and the ideals of sustainable tourism. The journey ahead is one of revelations, some of which may be unsettling, as we unravel the complexities clouding CNMI's tourism landscape.

Third World frameworks, often seen as a lifeline for developing regions, tend to conceal more than they reveal. The CNMI, like many territories and nations, has been drawn into the whirlwind of promises these frameworks offer. The immediate allure of economic growth often blinds regions to the deeper, systemic issues that lurk beneath the surface, threatening the islands' vibrant ecosystem and rich cultural heritage.

The temptation of quick financial gains has consistently swayed many regions operating within Third World frameworks. In the CNMI, a hasty effort ensued to monetize its natural wonders and cultural riches. While this might provide a short-term economic surge, it fails to account for long-term consequences. Once resources are exhausted or commercialized to the point of no return, they are lost, potentially leaving future generations without their natural treasures and cultural roots.

The appeal of immediate solutions, often proposed by external parties eager to tap into the CNMI's tourism market, tends to overshadow the essential need for sustainable, future-oriented planning. Infrastructure developments rise with scant regard for their ecological repercussions; tourism initiatives are rolled out with minimal genuine interaction with the indigenous communities. This approach, dictated by urgency rather than thoughtful deliberation, positions the CNMI to face many challenges – from the environment's fragility to the potential fading of its cultural essence.

The CNMI's entanglement with Third World frameworks has brought it to a precarious juncture, where the shimmering promises of economic progress clash with the stark realities of long-term sustainability. With its heavy lean towards immediate gratification, this imbalance has led the islands down a path where the exploitation of resources and cultural commodification have become distressingly commonplace. In a rush to satiate the ever-growing appetite for global tourism, the CNMI stands to lose more than it gains—sacrificing the essence that defines its allure. The need for a recalibration is clear: a shift towards practices that honor the intrinsic value of the islands' natural and cultural wealth, ensuring that their trajectory is not one of irreversible loss but of mindful and enduring prosperity.

The CNMI's entanglement in external economic ties has created a snare of reliance that binds the islands firmly to the tenets of Third World frameworks. This dependence, largely a consequence of foreign investments, arrives laden with conditions that veer the CNMI off the course of sustainable practices and onto tracks aligned with immediate, profit-centric aims.

With the CNMI's embrace of global investors, particularly from wealthier regions, it has inadvertently relinquished a slice of its autonomy. These investors, enticed by the prospects of substantial profits, often dictate terms and practices that place their economic gains above the environmental and cultural health of the islands. This dynamic gives rise to a modern form of subtle subjugation, where the CNMI retains its sovereignty in name but finds its course dictated by foreign economic currents.

This modern subjugation takes various forms, from resource distribution to shaping policies in crucial sectors such as tourism. In this skewed equation, the interests and needs of the local community are often overshadowed by the grand designs of international stakeholders. Amidst this imbalance, the indigenous people's concerns and aspirations for sustainable living are frequently muted by the louder narrative of economic expansion.

The ramifications of this economic dependency are significant. The CNMI is caught in a vortex where the chase for foreign investment overshadows the quest for sustainable practices. This vortex deepens the islands' reliance on outside economies, amplifies social disparities, and strains the delicate natural resources. If unaddressed, this pattern threatens to dismantle the unique fabric that defines the CNMI, leaving in its wake a milieu marred by exploitation and a culture diluted by outside forces.

Before the pandemic, the CNMI was a bustling hub for tourists seeking its idyllic shores and cultural splendor. However, this visitor surge brought a shadow that loomed over the islands' environment. The onslaught of over-tourism placed immense stress on natural resources, leaving visible scars on the once pristine environment.

The islands' delicate ecosystems, tailored over millennia to a harmonious balance, found themselves ill-equipped to handle the influx of tourists. Beaches that once boasted fine, untouched sands began to show signs of erosion and litter as the footfalls of countless visitors left an indelible mark. The coral reefs, vibrant with marine life, started to suffer from the consequences of over-exposure to human activity, with some areas showing signs of coral bleaching and habitat disruption.

The verdant forests, home to many species, faced the encroachment of development. Trails that once meandered gently through the woods became well-trodden paths, and the hum of tourism often drowned out the sounds of nature. The air, once crisp and clean, carried the faint but growing taint of pollution, a testament to the increasing environmental footprint of the tourism industry.

This period before the pandemic serves as a poignant reminder of the environmental cost of unbridled tourism. Grasping the consequences of over-tourism in its eagerness to welcome tourists, the CNMI stands as a stark warning of the delicate balance between natural preservation and economic exploitation—a balance that, once upset, can lead to irreversible damage. The pandemic's pause in tourism has provided a respite but also a moment of reflection on how to move forward sustainably, ensuring that past mistakes do not repeat in the future.

As the CNMI reflects on the environmental impact of its tourism boom, a parallel narrative emerges—one that is less visible but equally significant. The environmental degradation, a stark reminder of the tangible consequences of over-tourism, finds its counterpart in a more silent, yet profound, cultural shift. This transition from the ecological to the cultural landscape of the CNMI reveals a multifaceted crisis where the very soul of the islands—their rich traditions and cultural identity—is at risk of being overshadowed by external influences and commercialization. As we turn our attention from the damaged coral reefs and eroded beaches to the dilution of indigenous culture, the interconnectedness of these issues becomes apparent, underscoring the need for a holistic approach to the challenges facing the CNMI.

The CNMI's cultural landscape, rich with the traditions of the Chamorro and Carolinian people, faces a silent crisis. Over the years, the islands have witnessed a gradual overshadowing of their indigenous cultures, replaced in many instances by more popular Polynesian influences, particularly Hawaiian. Souvenirs and cultural representations have often leaned towards these more recognized traditions, leaving Chamorro and Carolinian heritage in the shadows.

This shift towards external cultural paradigms has diluted the authentic local experience for visitors. The CNMI, a melting pot of unique traditions, has struggled to showcase its cultural identity on the tourism stage. The lack of dedicated cultural centers exacerbates this issue, leaving tourists with limited opportunities to immerse themselves in the genuine Chamorro and Carolinian way of life.

As a result, the CNMI's cultural essence risks becoming a mere footnote in its tourism narrative. The islands' rich history and the vibrant living traditions of its indigenous people have not been given the spotlight they deserve. Instead, they are often relegated to occasional performances or seasonal events, failing to fully capture these cultures' depth and richness.

In the CNMI, the vibrant heritage of Chamorro and Carolinian traditions has often been outshone by the more globally known Hawaiian cultures. The islands now stand at a critical juncture, needing to reevaluate how they present their cultural wealth to the world. This is about safeguarding cultural identity and ensuring that the precious cultural heritage, inherited across generations, does not fade amidst the vastness of worldwide tourism.

The diverse difficulties encountered by the CNMI, ranging from the dilution of cultural identity to policy shortcomings, highlight a more extensive issue: The islands are struggling with the repercussions of policies and actions that have favored immediate economic benefits at the expense of enduring sustainability and cultural preservation. Examining the CNMI's policy framework more closely reveals that this focus on short-term gains, driven by local directives, has resulted in choices that threaten the islands' environmental, cultural, and economic longevity.

In the CNMI, government policies have historically mirrored the Third World paradigm, focusing on immediate economic upliftment, often at the expense of long-term sustainability. While yielding short-term gains, this myopic vision has set the stage for a host of long-term challenges that now threaten the fabric of the islands' future.

The focus on swift economic expansion frequently gives preference to projects and initiatives that promise immediate financial benefits. While boosting the economy in the short run, this approach has overlooked the necessity of integrating sustainability into the core of developmental strategies. Consequently, the islands have witnessed a proliferation of endeavors that, although economically lucrative, have sown the seeds for future ecological and cultural crises.

The absence of sustainability as a foundational principle in policy-making has manifested in various forms. Infrastructure projects have been greenlit without comprehensive environmental impact assessments, and tourism developments have proceeded with little regard for their long-term implications on local communities and natural habitats. These policy shortfalls have jeopardized the islands' environmental health and threatened to erode the cultural integrity that makes the CNMI unique.

The consequences of these policy shortfalls are becoming increasingly evident. Environmental degradation, cultural dilution, and economic vulnerabilities are challenges confronting the CNMI. The need for a fundamental policy shift is evident. A new paradigm that places sustainability at its heart is imperative for the CNMI to navigate the complex interplay of economic development, cultural preservation, and environmental stewardship.

The path forward demands a reimagining of policies, a move away from the narrow focus on immediate economic gains towards a more holistic approach that considers the welfare of future generations. This change necessitates embracing sustainability not merely as a supplementary consideration or a procedural formality but as the fundamental driving force behind all development initiatives. Only then can the CNMI hope to forge a prosperous, culturally rich, and environmentally sound future.

This situation sets the stage for a deeper inquiry into the very nature of the CNMI's development strategies. The islands' attempts to balance Third World frameworks and sustainable tourism have often resembled a high-wire act, fraught with instability and the risk of a significant fall. Despite intentions to harmonize these conflicting paradigms, the CNMI's efforts have frequently stumbled, revealing the fundamental discord between immediate economic pursuits and the ideals of long-term sustainability.

As we reflect on the CNMI's journey, the illusion of balance between the rapid development of Third World frameworks and the measured approach of sustainable tourism becomes increasingly apparent. It is a reflection that invites a critical examination of the systemic changes necessary to realign the islands' trajectory—one that acknowledges the complexities and embraces a future where economic vitality and sustainability are not mutually exclusive but are integrated into a harmonious and lasting union.

The quest to balance Third World frameworks and sustainable tourism in the CNMI has been akin to walking a tightrope—a delicate and often illusory endeavor. While there have been attempts to harmonize these divergent paradigms, they frequently fall short, mired in a fundamental mismatch of principles and objectives.

Third World frameworks, with their emphasis on rapid economic growth and development, often push for the maximization of short-term gains. This approach is characterized by aggressive tourism strategies, infrastructure expansion, and resource exploitation, all driven by the urgency to elevate economic standings. In contrast, sustainable tourism calls for a measured, conscientious approach that prioritizes long-term environmental health, cultural preservation, and equitable economic benefits.

Efforts to blend these models in the CNMI have often resulted in superficial adjustments—cosmetic changes that do little to address the underlying systemic disparities. Initiatives that appear sustainable on the surface may still operate within a framework that ultimately serves the immediate economic agenda, leaving the more profound tenets of sustainability unaddressed.

The inherent incompatibility of Third World frameworks and sustainable tourism is rooted in their divergent trajectories. One looks to immediate horizons, eager for rapid results; the other casts its gaze further, envisioning a future where growth and preservation coexist. The fallacy lies in believing that these models can be reconciled without profound systemic transformations—without reevaluating priorities, realigning policies, and a genuine commitment to sustainability principles.

In the CNMI, this illusion of balance has manifested in initiatives that, while commendable in intent, are insufficient in scope and depth. They often lack the structural support, policy coherence, and community integration necessary for genuine sustainability. Without these foundational elements, attempts at balance become precarious, threatening to topple under the weight of inherent contradictions.

As the CNMI continues its journey, the need for significant systemic changes becomes increasingly apparent. Only through a radical rethinking of development paradigms, a realignment of policies, and a deep-seated commitment to sustainable principles can a proper balance be achieved—a balance that serves the present and honors the future. This delicate equilibrium, vital for the CNMI's future, not only affects its present development strategies but also casts long shadows on what lies ahead. Without such pivotal changes, the CNMI stares into a future rife with uncertainties and challenges.

As we cast our gaze forward, the long-term implications of the CNMI's current trajectory become sharper. The islands, rich in natural beauty and cultural heritage, stand on the precipice of a future that could see these treasures irrevocably tarnished if the path remains unchanged. The warning signs are already evident: environmental degradation, cultural dilution, and economic fragility.

Continuing along this trajectory without a pivot toward sustainability poses many risks. The most immediate is the environmental impact. The CNMI's lush landscapes, diverse ecosystems, and vibrant coral reefs could face irreversible damage. This environmental decline would not only mar the natural beauty that the islands are renowned for but also disrupt the delicate balance of ecosystems upon which local communities and diverse wildlife depend.

From a cultural standpoint, the risk is just as profound. The gradual erosion of Chamorro and Carolinian traditions, already overshadowed by external influences, could accelerate, leading to a loss of cultural identity for which no economic gain can compensate. Once vibrant, the unique cultural fabric of the CNMI could fade into a pale imitation, replaced by a homogenized version tailored for tourist consumption.

Economically, the consequences are equally dire. Over-reliance on tourism, mainly when it follows unsustainable practices, creates a fragile economic foundation. The CNMI could find itself caught in a vicious cycle, where the aspects that attract tourists—the pristine environment and rich culture—are undermined. As these attractions diminish, so too could the flow of tourists, leading to economic instability.

Moving ahead demands a significant change towards a framework prioritizing long-term sustainability above immediate profits. This approach calls for an integrated strategy combining economic growth with environmental conservation and safeguarding cultural heritage. The enduring success of the CNMI depends on striking this equilibrium, guaranteeing the protection and prosperity of its natural and cultural treasures for future generations.

Without this pivot, the CNMI risks a future where its children inherit a land stripped of its natural wonders and a culture diluted beyond recognition. The decision is evident, and the moment to make a move is immediate. The CNMI's future hinges on the aspiration to make the right decision that leads to a sustainable and flourishing tomorrow. As we turn the page, this hope must fuel the CNMI's journey towards a harmonious balance between development and preservation, guiding its path into a sustainable tomorrow.

The way forward demands courage, innovation, and an unwavering commitment to sustainability principles. It requires the CNMI to forge partnerships that honor the islands' unique identity, craft policies that safeguard its environmental and cultural legacy, and pursue a resilient and forward-looking economic vision.

As this chapter concludes, it leaves a mosaic of insights and lessons, each underscoring the urgency of the task. For the CNMI, the time to act is now. The choices made today will echo through the corridors of its future, shaping the legacy it leaves for generations to come. The call is clear: to forge a path that harmonizes economic vitality with the enduring values of sustainability, ensuring that the beauty and richness of the CNMI endure far into the future.

Chapter 8

Decolonizing Tourism: Breaking Away from Elitist Paradigms

The Northern Mariana Islands, pivotal in the Pacific tourism industry, are etched with a complex history marked by colonial legacies and socio-economic upheavals. The tourism sector, while a cornerstone of economic prosperity, is intricately woven with strands of elitism—echoes of power imbalances that continue to influence the islands' trajectory. This chapter critically examines these traditional paradigms, shedding light on the entrenched structures of power and privilege that have long dictated the course of the CNMI's tourism narrative.

Embarking on a journey of decolonization, we aim to dismantle the established power dynamics that have favored a select few, often overshadowing the interests and voices of the local communities. This exploration reflects not only the sustainability and equity of the prevailing tourism model but also a clarion call for transformative change.

Decolonizing tourism in the CNMI is more than a theoretical pursuit; it is an actionable imperative. It involves redefining the tourism landscape to honor the islands' cultural richness, safeguard their environmental treasures, and ensure that the fruits of tourism are shared equitably among all community members. This shift advocates for a transition from focusing on immediate profit to long-term sustainability, from exclusionary practices to inclusive engagement, and from exploitative tendencies to empowerment.

Embarking on this chapter's journey, we must acknowledge that the pursuit of decolonizing tourism is a shared venture. It is a path that beckons us to deeply examine and comprehend the enduring patterns of elitism woven into the fabric of CNMI's contemporary tourism industry. A critical look at the sustained influence of the elite in steering tourism policies, juxtaposed with the escalating disparity between their agendas and the aspirations of local communities, allows us to dissect the intricate tapestry of dominance and power within the sector. This insight is not just pivotal but foundational, as it propels us toward a more nuanced exploration of the nuances of elitism in today's CNMI tourism. This exploration will illuminate the steps necessary for a genuine decolonization of tourism.

In the contemporary tourism landscape of the CNMI, the imprints of elitism are unmistakable, manifesting prominently in the decision-making processes that shape the industry. The elite, an amalgam of influential political figures, affluent business owners, and individuals with deep-rooted societal connections, continue to wield significant power. Their decisions resonate through the archipelago, often determining the trajectory of tourism development and its associated outcomes.

This elite dominance is evident in the allocation of resources, the prioritization of specific projects over others, and the framing of policies that disproportionately benefit the upper echelons of society. Investment in opulent resorts, exclusive attractions, and high-end facilities often takes precedence, driven by the expectation of hefty returns. While contributing to the islands' allure as a premium destination, these developments often sideline the broader interests of local communities and the environment.

The clout of the elite in tourism decision-making is also visible in the legislative realm. Policies and regulations are frequently tailored to accommodate the interests of those at the top, occasionally at the expense of sustainable practices and equitable economic distribution. The consequences of this imbalanced approach are varied, affecting not just the ecological equilibrium but also the societal structure of the CNMI.

Recently, the gap between the elite's priorities and the community's needs has become more evident. The elite's focus on profit and status frequently neglects the desires and welfare of the residents. While economically lucrative, large-scale developments can lead to displacement, cultural commodification, and environmental degradation – issues that directly affect the community but are frequently marginalized in boardrooms and policy discussions.

The community's needs extend beyond economic prospects to include the conservation of cultural heritage, environmental care, and social unity. Nevertheless, these essential aspects are frequently eclipsed by the ambitious plans of the elite, whose choices are mainly driven by financial considerations and the pursuit of global competitiveness.

This exploration of the elite's dominance and it's disconnecting with community needs in modern CNMI tourism draws to a close, paving the way for a deeper reflection. It is crucial to acknowledge that the journey toward a decolonized, inclusive, and sustainable tourism industry is complex and challenging. The task ahead involves policy changes and a fundamental shift in the power dynamics and perspectives that have long governed the industry. The voices of the community must be heard and their needs addressed, ensuring that the future development of tourism in the CNMI is anchored in sustainability and equity. Only by taking such transformative actions can the CNMI aspire to navigate a new direction, moving away from entrenched elitist models towards a future that values inclusiveness and comprehensive development.

In an era increasingly conscious of past imbalances and injustices, decolonization has become more prominent, urging societies to re-evaluate and adjust the impacts of their colonial history. Within tourism, particularly in places like the CNMI with its colonial past, decolonization is not merely a theoretical construct but a practical imperative. It involves peeling away the layers of historical dominance and power imbalances to create an inclusive, equitable tourism model that reflects indigenous cultures and communities.

At its core, decolonization in tourism is about recentering the local communities' narratives, experiences, and priorities that colonial legacies and elitist models have marginalized. It calls for a tourism industry that acknowledges and actively integrates these communities' voices and visions into its framework. This means moving away from a model that views destinations merely as commodities for consumption and towards one that respects and celebrates the inherent value of places and their people.

Decolonization in tourism also involves dismantling the structures and practices perpetuating inequality and exploitation. It questions the paradigms prioritizing profit over people, commodifying cultures for entertainment, and valuing external perceptions over internal realities. Instead, it advocates for a sustainable and respectful model collaboratively developed with the communities it aims to benefit.

The tourism industry in the CNMI, similar to others, is influenced by an elitist framework that centralizes power and profits among a select few, often neglecting the broader needs of the local community and the environment. This approach has led to various issues, including environmental damage, the commodification of culture, and economic disparities. Changing this strategy is essential, not just from a moral or ethical perspective but also for practical considerations. The sustained success of the tourism sector in locations like the CNMI relies on its capacity to embrace more sustainable and fair practices.

Shifting away from elitist models means rethinking how tourism is developed, marketed, and managed. It requires an inclusive approach that engages local communities as equal partners rather than passive beneficiaries or mere spectators. It also necessitates a reassessment of what constitutes success in the tourism industry. Instead of measuring success solely through economic metrics, a decolonized approach would also consider social and environmental impacts, cultural integrity, and community well-being.

Embracing decolonization in tourism is a complex task. It challenges entrenched power structures and requires a willingness to change long-standing practices. However, the advantages of making this shift are significant. It promotes a more just and balanced industry while enriching the tourism experience, offering travelers a deeper and more genuine connection with the destinations they visit. For places like the CNMI and other destinations worldwide grappling with similar issues, the commitment to a transformative journey is essential for cultivating an industry that is truly reflective of and beneficial to the local communities it represents.

In the verdant realms of the CNMI, a struggle for narrative control simmers beneath the surface. The Chamorro and Carolinian communities, guardians of a rich cultural heritage, are in a relentless tug-of-war against an industry that has often overlooked their voices. Within the shadows of the tourism sector, dominated by a local elite with vested interests, the genuine narratives of these indigenous communities are frequently stifled, their perspectives sidelined.

For far too long, the Chamorro and Carolinian people have witnessed the commercialization of their culture, their homelands packaged as commodities in the tourism marketplace. Their sacred traditions and sites are marketed to tourists without consent or accurate representation, reducing profound cultural symbols to mere tourist attractions. Calls for inclusivity and authentic representation in the industry have often been disregarded, as the elite, entrenched in their positions of power, continue to gatekeep the industry's decision-making processes.

The reality is stark — in the corridors of power where tourism policies are crafted, the voices of the Chamorro and Carolinian communities are conspicuously absent. Guided by a handful of leaders, the industry appears to function in isolation, detached from the communities whose culture it monetizes. This has caused a noticeable feeling of marginalization among the indigenous populations, who have repeatedly sought a more active involvement in the industry, only to be consistently overlooked.

In the face of such exclusion, stories of resistance emerge. They are tales not of triumph but of ongoing battles against developments that threaten to uproot their way of life. They speak of resilience, a culture fighting for survival against the relentless tide of commercialization. Community-led initiatives that seek to create alternative, sustainable tourism models often struggle to find footing in an industry where the elite hold the reins.

The situation paints a grim picture of a tourism industry deeply entrenched in elitism, where the local communities are seen not as partners but as bystanders, their cultural heritage exploited without due regard for their rights and voices. The Chamorro and Carolinian communities find themselves at a pivotal juncture, balancing the wish to showcase their vibrant cultural heritage to the world against the concern of additional cultural erosion by an industry commodifying their traditions and lifestyles.

As the story progresses, it is evident that the journey towards a just and inclusive tourism industry is filled with challenges. This path requires acknowledging the issue and a dedicated effort to dismantle the systems that continue to promote this exclusion. The quest for a tourism industry that genuinely respects and celebrates the Chamorro and Carolinian cultures is daunting, especially when faced with the might of an elite that seems indifferent to the voices of those they claim to represent.

Drawing lessons from different corners of the world, the narratives of New Zealand and Bhutan stand out as striking examples of how tourism can be reshaped to be more inclusive.

Consider New Zealand, where the indigenous Māori culture is not merely a tourist highlight but a living testament to a collaborative approach. The government and the Māori communities have come together to ensure their heritage is displayed and forms a vital and respected element of any visitor's journey (2018). This collaboration has ushered in fresh economic opportunities for the Māori, subtly redistributing power away from solely the tourism moguls.

On the other hand, Bhutan offers a unique model led by its philosophy of Gross National Happiness. Instead of mass tourism, Bhutan emphasizes quality over quantity, ensuring the perks of tourism are widespread rather than concentrated in the hands of a select few (2019). This approach safeguards their environment, ensures that their culture thrives, and that the economic benefits are evenly distributed.

New Zealand and Bhutan's strategies highlight the potential of creating a tourism industry that values every stakeholder. For the CNMI, these tales offer inspiration and a roadmap towards a more inclusive and equitable tourism landscape.

It is an ambitious undertaking to reimagine the CNMI's tourism industry as a domain that genuinely honors its cultural richness and listens to its community's voices. This journey from an elitist framework to one that embodies representation and fairness necessitates a radical transformation of deep-rooted structures and practices.

At the heart of this transformative journey lie community-led initiatives, which are instrumental in integrating the collective wisdom, cultural richness, and aspirations of the CNMI's inhabitants into the tourism narrative. Coalitions comprising local artisans, storytellers, environmental advocates, and other community members can offer a more authentic and respectful depiction of the islands' heritage within the tourism experience. These grassroots movements redefine industry success, placing greater value on cultural exchange and enriching experiences rather than solely on financial gain.

In parallel, a steadfast commitment to inclusivity is essential. This ensures that every voice, mainly those historically sidelined, is acknowledged and respected. Initiatives may range from providing platforms for youth to articulate their vision for the future to ensuring that tourism infrastructure is accessible to everyone. Such an inclusive approach celebrates diversity, allowing everyone to contribute to and benefit from the tourism industry.

However, the full potential of these community-led efforts and inclusive practices can only be realized with a solid framework of policy changes and legal reforms. This may entail re-examining and potentially amending regulations related to land utilization, environmental protection, and the framework of the tourism sector itself. Legal changes should strive to improve local community involvement in decision-making and guarantee that development initiatives align with the community's aspirations for sustainable and conscientious tourism.

Revamping governance structures is also crucial to democratize the decision-making process. This might entail restructuring tourism boards to reflect the community's diversity more accurately, increasing transparency, and fostering accountability. Such policy reforms provide the foundation for a more equitable tourism industry that generates economic prosperity while preserving cultural integrity and environmental sustainability.

The transformation of the CNMI's tourism industry towards a more equitable and inclusive model also offers hope for newly minted college graduates. This transition offers numerous prospects for these young professionals, not just to join the workforce but to establish significant and satisfying careers. To ensure the industry thrives in line with decolonization values, creating well-paid, fulfilling career opportunities for these graduates is crucial.

The new paradigm should focus on creating a diverse array of job opportunities that extend beyond traditional roles. Graduates with degrees in environmental science could be employed to spearhead sustainability initiatives. At the same time, those with a background in cultural studies might be tasked with curating authentic experiences that celebrate the CNMI's rich heritage. Marketing graduates could find their niche in promoting the islands in ways that honor their history and culture, and hospitality majors could help reshape the service industry to reflect local customs and values.

The industry, aiming to attract and retain a talented pool of graduates, must provide competitive pay scales that acknowledge their academic accomplishments and the crucial role they will play in shaping CNMI's tourism future. Clear career progression pathways should also be established, allowing graduates to ascend through the industry ranks. This could involve mentorship programs, ongoing professional development, and opportunities for leadership roles.

Incorporating these elements into the CNMI's tourism industry provides a robust platform for college graduates' personal and professional growth. It injects fresh perspectives and innovative ideas into the sector. This approach guarantees that the industry benefits from the insights of experience while invigorating the enthusiasm and innovation of the younger generation. Maintaining this equilibrium is essential for nurturing an industry that is dynamic, robust, and progressive, adept at adjusting to the changing dynamics of international tourism while adhering to the principles of decolonization.

In essence, decolonizing CNMI's tourism is a multifaceted endeavor, intertwining the vigor and innovation of community initiatives with the strategic direction of thoughtful policy reform. It is a harmonious blend of grassroots enthusiasm and systemic transformation, each reinforcing the other, collectively steering the CNMI towards an economically vibrant, socially responsible, and culturally enriching tourism industry.

We must acknowledge the possible roadblocks as we contemplate the progressive strategies and initiatives designed to decolonize CNMI's tourism industry. Transitioning towards a more inclusive and equitable model is fraught with challenges that must be navigated with caution and resolve.

The journey toward decolonizing tourism in the CNMI is not without its challenges. At the forefront is the resistance from established elites who have long held sway over the industry. Their vested interests and entrenched power positions often make them averse to changes threatening their status quo. Convincing these influential figures to embrace a more equitable and inclusive model, or at least to not actively obstruct it, is a daunting task that requires tactful negotiation and persistent advocacy.

Furthermore, balancing the immediate economic needs of the CNMI with the long-term goals of cultural and environmental preservation presents a delicate tightrope walk. While tourism is an essential source of income for the islands, adhering to conventional models may result in the overuse and depletion of resources. Finding a middle ground that ensures economic stability without compromising the CNMI's cultural heritage and natural beauty is crucial.

While these challenges are formidable, they are not insurmountable. Through unified efforts from all parties involved, a well-defined strategy, and a dedication to sustainable and inclusive methods, the CNMI can surmount these obstacles and create a profitable tourism sector mindful of its diverse cultural heritage and natural surroundings.

As we delve into the complexities and potential stumbling blocks in the journey toward a decolonized tourism industry in the CNMI, it is crucial to maintain a balanced perspective. Recognizing the inherent challenges is just as important as identifying the opportunities.

The path to implementing change in the CNMI's tourism sector is strewn with resistance and challenges. Navigating the intricacies of entrenched power dynamics and overcoming resistance from those who benefit from the status quo requires resilience and strategic thinking. Change agents must be prepared to confront skepticism, counteract inertia, and address the fears of those wary of transformation.

Nevertheless, within these challenges lie significant opportunities for sustainable and inclusive growth. By leveraging the rich cultural heritage and pristine natural environment of the CNMI, there is potential to develop a tourism model that is unique, attractive, ethical, and responsible. This approach can create a more diversified and resilient economy, offering a broader range of stakeholders the chance to participate and benefit.

Embracing these opportunities demands a shift in mindset and a willingness to explore innovative solutions. It involves engaging with local communities, fostering partnerships, and learning from global best practices. With the right blend of determination and creativity, the CNMI can turn these challenges into stepping stones, paving the way for a tourism industry that is both prosperous and principled.

As we pivot from acknowledging the challenges and embracing the opportunities, our focus now turns to the horizon, where a vision of a decolonized and equitable tourism industry in the CNMI beckons. It is a vision that requires imagination and actionable steps to bring it to fruition.

Picturing a future for the CNMI's tourism that is both decolonized and fair calls for a reimagining of the islands. It is a future where the vibrant tapestry of local culture, the pristine allure of nature, and the invigorating essence of community life are not merely safeguarded but actively revered and shared with the world conscientiously. This envisaged future sees tourism transformed from one-sided to reciprocal, dignified, and mutually beneficial encounters between those who visit and call these islands home.

Bringing this envisioned future into reality necessitates the establishment of a pathway comprised of intentional actions. This begins with a deep-seated commitment to authentically involving the community and bolstering its capacity to steer and prosper from the evolution of tourism. This trajectory entails nurturing the educational and professional prowess of the local populace, ensuring they possess the competencies and tools necessary to navigate and thrive within the tourism sector. In tandem, a recalibration of policies, strategic infrastructure development, and a reorientation of promotional efforts are imperative, all gravitating towards a future that honors sustainability, equity, and the preservation of cultural authenticity.

This envisaged future is far from a figment of imagination; it is an attainable reality that can be materialized through dedicated collective action, strategic alliances, and an unwavering dedication to equity and righteousness. With every progressive stride, we edge closer to a tourism industry that does not just operate within the CNMI but resonates with its core values, hopes, and the very soul of its communities.

Chapter 9

Evaluating the TRIP Initiative: A Critical Analysis of CNMI's Multimillion-Dollar Tourism Strategy and Its Economic Implications

The Tourism Resumption Investment Plan (TRIP), an initiative by the CNMI government, was developed as a strategic response to the global travel downturn caused by the COVID-19 pandemic. Recognizing the critical role of tourism in the economy, the CNMI committed a significant sum of $15 million to each of its key markets, South Korea and Japan (Erediano, 2023). This move was intended to jumpstart the recovery and revitalization of the tourism sector, which the pandemic had severely impacted.

In its initial phase, the TRIP program focused on South Korea, capitalizing on the travel bubble agreement to stimulate targeted economic activity. The program implemented an innovative approach, providing South Korean tourists with 'Travel Bucks' ranging from $250 to $500 per visitor for each island of Saipan, Tinian, and Rota (MVA, 2021). This initiative aimed to boost local spending, benefiting various businesses, including optional tour operators, retail stores, and restaurants, thereby injecting vitality into the local economy.

Furthermore, the TRIP program's comprehensive strategy included airline subsidies and support for travel agents, hotels, and qualified local businesses (MVA, 2021). This multifaceted approach was designed to ensure continued air connectivity, vital for the arrival of tourists, and to stimulate broader economic activity within the CNMI. This strategic decision reflects a comprehensive approach to reinvigorating the tourism sector by addressing various facets of the travel and hospitality industry.

The expansion of the TRIP program to include Japan, a vital market for CNMI's tourism, marked a significant shift in strategy. The program for Japan was focused on incentivizing airlines, travel agencies, and local businesses (Limol, 2022). It included subsidies for airlines operating at less than 40% capacity to maintain air connectivity, crucial for attracting Japanese tourists (Staf, 2021). Additionally, the program encompassed various marketing programs tailored to resonate with the Japanese market (Esmores, 2022). The TRIP initiative's efforts were crucial in revitalizing the tourism-dependent economy of CNMI. They focused on attracting a key segment of travelers while explicitly addressing the unique dynamics of the Japanese market.

Implementing the CNMI's TRIP program, which focused on subsidies, was intended to rapidly rejuvenate the region's tourism sector. However, this approach was significantly flawed due to its short-term focus. While these subsidies aimed to provide immediate support, particularly to airlines based outside the CNMI and hotels linked to off-island investors, they lacked a vision for sustainable, long-term growth in the local tourism industry.

When evaluating the program's outcomes, the disconnect between the substantial financial investment and the actual results becomes apparent. Although there was a marginal increase in tourist arrivals due to the program's incentives, this did not correspond to a sustainable increase in tourism or justify the investment's scale. Moreover, the economic impact of these measures predominantly benefited external entities, leaving the local economy with minimal long-term benefits.

In its Japan-oriented segment, the CNMI's TRIP program included a subsidy provision for airlines operating at less than 40% capacity. However, the program did not yield the expected results, as evidenced in the first two months, when flight load factors from Japan to CNMI hovered around 30% (Esmores, 2022). This situation, where the airlines frequently qualified for subsidies, revealed a significant shortfall in the program's effectiveness. The outcomes highlight the complexities in attracting Japanese tourists post-pandemic, suggesting CNMI needs to reevaluate and adapt its market strategies to better align with the Japanese audience's specific travel behaviors and preferences.

In the South Korean segment of the TRIP program, while Travel Bucks were exclusively available for spending within the CNMI, contributing to the local economy, other aspects of the program, like airline subsidies and travel agent support, primarily benefited entities based in Korea. This was due to the arrangement where airline tickets and travel agent services were predominantly procured within Korea. This structure led to a significant part of the intended economic stimulus for CNMI's tourism sector circulating externally, underscoring a strategic misalignment in retaining the total economic impact.

The execution of the TRIP program notably lacked crucial aspects of sustainable tourism development, such as comprehensive market analysis and long-term planning. This shortfall led to a temporary boost in tourism, failing to establish a long-lasting, beneficial trajectory for CNMI's tourism sector. As a result, while the program succeeded in creating a temporary surge in tourism, it fell short of fostering a sustainable trajectory for CNMI's tourism sector. This led to a situation where the anticipated revitalization of tourism transformed into a short-lived phenomenon, lacking significant long-term benefits for the local community and economy.

When critically analyzed, the TRIP program's financial efficacy reveals a concerning narrative of misplaced priorities and underwhelming outcomes. Backed by substantial investments in the millions, there were high expectations that the program would significantly boost tourist arrivals and rejuvenate the economy. However, the actual outcomes were notably different from these expectations. The vast sums allocated for boosting the tourism sector seemed disproportionate compared to the influx of tourists and the resultant economic activity. This mismatch raises questions about the program's strategic financial planning and ability to deliver a meaningful return on investment.

The response to the TRIP program further underscores its limitations in the key markets of South Korea and Japan. While the program included a travel bubble agreement with South Korea, the anticipated flood of tourists from this market did not materialize as expected. The incentives offered, though attractive on paper, failed to drive up the number of visitors from South Korea significantly. Similarly, despite considerable promotional efforts and additional funding in Japan, the program did not achieve the desired breakthrough in attracting Japanese tourists. The lackluster response from these markets, crucial to the program's success, points to a fundamental disconnect between the TRIP program's offerings and international travelers' evolving preferences and behaviors in the post-pandemic world.

The financial efficacy of the TRIP program and its market response in South Korea and Japan paint a picture of an initiative that, despite its grand scale and significant financial backing, fell short of achieving its primary objectives. The program's focus on short-term, immediate gains overlooked the nuances of sustainable tourism development and failed to resonate effectively with its target markets. This led to a scenario where the investment in the TRIP program did not translate into the envisaged economic rejuvenation for the CNMI, leaving much to be desired in terms of strategic effectiveness and long-term economic benefits.

The TRIP program's approach, marked by focusing on short-term recovery through subsidies and incentives, lacked critical elements for long-term sustainability in the tourism sector. This approach neglected the integration of initiatives that could foster ongoing tourism growth, such as investing in local tourism infrastructure, community-based tourism projects, or sustainable tourism practices. These oversights call into question the program's long-term viability and strategic foresight. While it succeeded in creating a temporary influx of tourists, it failed to establish a framework for enduring growth, overlooking the evolving global trends in tourism, especially the increasing emphasis on sustainable and responsible travel.

A closer examination of the TRIP program's economic benefits distribution reveals a skewed pattern favoring specific stakeholders. Most financial benefits flowed to airlines based outside the CNMI and larger hotel chains, often linked to off-island investors. This allocation led to a significant portion of the program's funds benefiting entities beyond the local economy.

The disparities in benefit allocation had profound implications for local businesses. Small and medium enterprises, crucial to CNMI's tourism ecosystem, were largely overlooked. This uneven distribution questions the program's equity and highlights a missed opportunity to foster a more inclusive economic growth model. Local businesses, crucial for driving sustainable tourism development, were sidelined, resulting in a concentration of benefits among a few rather than a widespread economic uplift.

Considering the challenges identified in the TRIP program, it becomes clear that future tourism initiatives should pivot towards a more strategic, long-term approach. This means developing plans that address immediate needs and incorporate sustainability principles to support the local economy and protect the environment over time. Central to this approach is redirecting a substantial portion of tourism revenue back into the local community, mainly supporting small and medium-sized businesses. These businesses are the lifeblood of sustainable economic growth, and by nurturing them, tourism can become a more effective tool for widespread economic development. By focusing on these areas, future strategies can create a more balanced and enduring tourism sector that benefits visitors and residents alike.

Moreover, detailed market research should be the foundation of any future strategy, ensuring the initiatives are closely tailored to different target markets' preferences and trends. Emphasizing sustainable and responsible tourism practices will align with global travel trends and ensure the preservation of CNMI's natural and cultural assets. Furthermore, it is crucial to coordinate to distribute tourism's economic advantages more evenly, ensuring that local communities and enterprises obtain a just portion of the profits.

In conclusion, despite its shortcomings, the TRIP program offers valuable lessons for future tourism and economic policies in the CNMI. This emphasizes the significance of embracing a comprehensive and future-oriented strategy in tourism advancement, ensuring harmony between short-term economic benefits and enduring sustainability and inclusiveness. The program's experiences suggest a necessary shift in tourism strategies towards reviving the economy and sustaining it resiliently, ensuring that the benefits are widely distributed and aligned with evolving global tourism trends and environmental considerations. As such, the TRIP program serves as both a learning point and a catalyst for reimagining the future of tourism in the CNMI, steering it towards a more sustainable, inclusive, and prosperous path.

Chapter 10

Impact of Digital Evolution and Technological Innovation on Tourism

In the continuously evolving landscape of our global environment, the digital revolution has stood out as a transformative force, redefining the dynamics of industries across the spectrum. The tourism sector, a vibrant collage of cultural exchanges and experiences, has been significantly influenced by this wave of change. This chapter seeks to unravel the profound impact of digital evolution and technological innovation on tourism, reimagining the industry from its core.

The onset of the digital age has marked the beginning of a new time of exceptional interconnectedness, making the vast world reachable with just a click. The way we discover, encounter, and interact with various places has been transformed by new technologies, changing the essence of travel itself. From the planning phases to the culmination of a journey, technology has become an indispensable travel companion, guiding, enhancing, and personalizing the traveler's experience. Recognizing the historical backdrop of this digital transformation is crucial. This transformation was gradual, transitioning from traditional travel agencies to the ubiquitous online platforms of today. Significant milestones have marked this evolution, heralding a step towards the digitization of tourism.

Today, the landscape is notably different. Travelers no longer rely solely on travel agents or brochures for information; they turn to the internet, an extensive repository of knowledge encompassing reviews, ratings, and immersive content. The industry's power dynamics have shifted, placing more control and autonomy in the hands of the traveler, democratizing access to travel experiences that were once the privilege of a select few.

The implications of this digital revolution are comprehensive and multifaceted, influencing how we travel and how destinations market themselves, how experiences are curated, and how the industry operates at its core. As we delve into the subsequent sections, we will unravel the myriad ways technological innovations have reshaped tourism, their challenges, and the opportunities they offer for a more sustainable, inclusive, and dynamic future for the industry.

The journey of digital innovation within the tourism industry is a fascinating saga of transformation and progress. In the late 20th century, a technological breakthrough was set to transform our interaction and understanding of the world. The traditional travel agency reigned supreme during this era, providing holidaymakers with expertly curated journeys via glossy brochures and bespoke services. These agencies stood as the pillars of travel wisdom, guiding the globe-trotters through the intricacies of voyaging across borders. With the internet's growth came a gradual yet profound integration into the tourism industry's fabric. The dawn of the 21st century marked a pivotal shift as the first online travel platforms debuted. With their user-friendly interfaces and comprehensive services, these platforms began to challenge traditional agencies' dominance. The newfound capability to effortlessly browse destinations, compare offerings, and seamlessly book trips online transformed the travel paradigm.

The rise of Web 2.0, defined by its interactivity and emphasis on user-generated content, propelled this transformation further (Kenton, 2023). Platforms like Trip Advisor and Yelp became treasure troves of insights, providing authentic reviews and recommendations from fellow travelers. Concurrently, the advent of social media turned every voyager into a storyteller, sharing their escapades and insights with a global audience. The proliferation of mobile technology ensured that the internet transcended the confines of desktops. Smartphones and tablets became vital travel accessories, acting as guides, interpreters, and digital journals. How we planned and lived out our travel experiences was being redefined, now conveniently nestled in the palm of our hands. The digital transformation that grips the tourism industry today is not a mere evolution but a groundbreaking leap into a new era of possibilities. Traditional travel agencies, which once stood unchallenged, now coexist with various online platforms, each offering distinctive services and experiences. From the initial spark of a travel idea to the cherished act of sharing memories, digital technology now permeates every facet of our travel experiences.

In a time characterized by swift technological advancements, tourism is not merely keeping up but actively harnessing these innovations. These technological developments are not just sophisticated tools; they are reshaping the very nature of travel, providing novel methods to explore, interact, and experience. Let us explore some of the pioneering technologies that are transforming tourism:

Mobile Technologies: Our smartphones serve as guides, translators, and ticket booths, all combined into a compact device that easily fits our pockets. Apps have become indispensable travel buddies, whether for finding the best local eats or snagging last-minute hotel deals. Mobile boarding passes and check-ins have made airport queues a thing of the past, and digital wallets have simplified payments, making currency exchange woes a distant memory.

Virtual and Augmented Reality: These technologies are like magic lenses that transform the world around us. Virtual Reality (VR) allows us to teleport to distant destinations from our living rooms, offering sneak peeks of places we dream of visiting (Sheldon, 2022). Augmented Reality (AR) layers digital information onto the real world, turning a simple walk down the street into an interactive history lesson (Hayes, 2023). These immersive tools enhance the travel experience and make planning and decision-making more informed and fun.

Artificial Intelligence and Machine Learning: Artificial Intelligence (AI) and Machine Learning (ML) have revolutionized the travel industry as the unseen orchestrator of personalized and intuitive travel experiences. AI functions like a digital concierge, subtly shaping our journeys to align with our preferences (Koteshov, 2023). It employs sophisticated chatbots, available 24/7, to efficiently address our inquiries (2023). Simultaneously, it leverages advanced algorithms to craft travel recommendations that resonate with our tastes and historical preferences (2023). Beyond enhancing the customer-facing side of travel, AI plays a crucial role in streamlining operational aspects. It adeptly manages complex tasks such as predicting flight demands and optimizing hotel operations, ensuring a seamless intersection of convenience and efficiency in travel and tourism (2023).

Blockchain: This is the behind-the-scenes hero of the travel tech revolution. Blockchain's superpower lies in its ability to make transactions transparent, secure, and swift (Tamplin, 2023). It is like a digital ledger everyone trusts, paving the way for smoother bookings, more reliable reviews, and loyalty programs.

These innovations are more than just conveniences; they are transforming the essence of travel. They are making the world smaller, more accessible, and infinitely more fascinating. These technological innovations are also reshaping the travel trends.

In the contemporary digital era, platforms like Instagram, Facebook, TikTok, and Twitter have transformed communication and play a crucial role in shaping travel trends and decisions, making the impact of social media on the tourism industry substantial. A single post, a captivating photo, or a viral video can inspire wanderlust and influence travel choices. Social media has democratized travel inspiration. No longer reliant on glossy brochures or travel agents for ideas, potential travelers now turn to their feeds, where a kaleidoscope of destinations comes alive through the experiences of friends, influencers, and strangers alike. These platforms have become digital showcases of personal travel stories, each post a vignette into a new adventure, a hidden gem, or a must-visit locale. In addition, the allure of 'Instagrammable' spots has even led to new tourist hotspots, previously overlooked but now thronging with visitors eager to capture their shareable moments.

Moreover, social media has elevated the importance of peer reviews and recommendations. A positive review or a shared experience from a trusted source can sway decisions more effectively than any advertisement. Travelers are increasingly seeking authentic experiences, and the candid insights provided by other travelers on social media platforms often serve as a more reliable guide than traditional marketing materials. For destinations and businesses, social media offers a dynamic and interactive platform for marketing and engagement. It provides a space to craft compelling narratives, showcase unique experiences, and interact directly with potential visitors. Engaging content can go viral, exponentially increasing reach and impact, while targeted advertising allows for precise audience segmentation. However, the influence of social media also brings challenges. The pursuit of 'like-worthy' experiences can lead to overcrowding and environmental strain on popular sites. There is also the risk of distorted expectations, as the curated perfection depicted online may not always align with reality. This places a responsibility on destinations and businesses to manage the impact of this digital influence thoughtfully. Social media has transformed tourism into a more accessible and inclusive domain, which has led to a new phenomenon: the democratization of travel.

Gone are the days when travel was a luxury reserved for the affluent few. The surge of digital technology has democratized the travel experience, making it a more achievable aspiration for a broader swath of society. For example, online platforms and user-friendly apps have emerged as game-changers, tearing down the financial and informational barriers that once made travel seem out of reach for many. Also, comparison sites and online bookings have returned the power to the traveler, allowing for a more personalized, budget-friendly journey. This newfound accessibility has opened the world to individuals from all walks of life, offering a glimpse into cultures and destinations that were once just distant dreams. In addition, platforms like Airbnb and Uber have provided more economical choices and a taste of authenticity, connecting travelers with local experiences that traditional avenues might miss.

Moreover, blogs, forums, and social media platforms have become indispensable sources, offering travelers the necessary information for self-guided global exploration. Nevertheless, this democratization brings forth its unique set of difficulties. The shadow of over-tourism looms, threatening the very destinations that technology has helped us discover. With greater accessibility comes greater responsibility—to travel sustainably and be mindful of the places we visit.

So, how can we use technology to explore, protect and preserve? Sustainable tourism and technology will intersect, paving the way for a future where travel is not only accessible but also conscientious and respectful of our world's precious resources. In the vanguard of modern travel, sustainable tourism and technology have allied, reinforcing the other's mission to protect our planet while exploring its wonders. This collaboration has given rise to a new form of tourism that is both mindful of the environment and economically and socially sustainable. The emergence of technology has equipped us with the means to reduce our ecological impact while we travel. For example, mobile apps that promote eco-friendly accommodations and green travel tips are just the tip of the iceberg.

Furthermore, platforms dedicated to carbon offsetting allow travelers to compensate for their flights' environmental impact with a few simple clicks. Furthermore, integrating renewable energy and innovative technology into the infrastructure of hotels and resorts is setting new standards for sustainability in the hospitality industry. From solar-powered lodgings to AI-driven energy management systems, technology is helping reduce waste and conserve resources in remarkable ways.

Beyond the ecological aspect, technology also empowers local communities by promoting responsible tourism that directly benefits them. Online marketplaces and social media platforms provide artisans and small tour operators with a global audience, enabling them to showcase authentic experiences that support the local economy and preserve cultural heritage.

However, as we chart this promising intersection of sustainable tourism and technology, it is crucial to remain vigilant. While a powerful enabler, technology must be wielded with care, ensuring that it serves as a bridge to a more sustainable future rather than a band-aid for unsustainable practices.

As transformative as it has been, the digital revolution in tourism has its pitfalls. The same technologies that have revolutionized the industry also present unique challenges and risks that require careful navigation. A primary concern in this context is safeguarding data privacy and security. Personal information accumulates significantly as travel services become more digitalized, from reservations to on-site experiences. Ensuring the protection of this data against breaches and misuse is crucial, yet it is an ongoing challenge amidst advanced cyber threats.

Furthermore, the dependence on technology can intensify the digital divide, leading to a significant gap between those without access to digital tools. This divide can appear in different forms, ranging from discrepancies between developed and developing areas to age-related divides within communities. Ensuring equitable access to the benefits of digital tourism is a challenge that must be met with intention and innovation. Another concern is that technological advancements might lead to unforeseen complications that overshadow or even replace the human element of travel. While automation and AI can enhance efficiency and personalization, they should be distinct from the authentic interactions and experiences at travel's heart. Preserving the warmth and richness of human connection in an increasingly digital world is a delicate balance. Finally, the ecological footprint of technology itself must be considered. The infrastructure that supports our digital world, from data centers to communication networks, consumes energy and resources. As we advocate for sustainable tourism, we must consider the sustainability of the technologies we employ and strive towards greener solutions.

While navigating the path of digital evolution in the tourism sector, addressing these challenges and risks is not just a choice but an absolute necessity. This journey demands vigilance, adaptability, and a dedication to sustainable approaches. Only through these efforts can we unlock the complete potential of technology to shape a tourism industry that is pioneering and inclusive but also ethical and robust.

Exploring the interplay of technology and tourism necessitates carefully examining real-world examples. These examples serve as both inspiration and cautionary learning grounds. They highlight the successes and pitfalls of integrating technology into the tourism industry, offering valuable insights into its future.

Many destinations have had successful experiences incorporating technology into the tourism industry. The first success story is about Singapore's model of smart tourism. Singapore's journey towards becoming a 'Smart Nation' is a commendable example. Singapore has leveraged data analytics, the Internet of Things (IoT), and artificial intelligence (AI) to significantly improve visitor experiences and operational efficiency within its tourism sector. Notable instances include implementing smart hotel rooms that adapt to guests' preferences and deploying real-time crowd management systems at popular tourist destinations (2023) (Utomo, 2020). These innovative applications of technology highlight the transformative potential of integrating digital solutions into tourism, creating experiences that are not only smooth but also tailored to individual preferences.

Another noteworthy example is Rwanda's pioneering approach to eco-tourism through technology. Rwanda has leveraged technology to promote eco-tourism and wildlife preservation. Using drones for wildlife monitoring and habitat mapping in its national parks has strengthened conservation initiatives while offering tourists a unique glimpse into Rwanda's diverse biodiversity (Frąckiewicz, 2023). However, despite these success stories, integrating technology into the tourism sector presents its share of challenges.

An illustration of this is Venice, Italy. The surge of visitors, partly attributed to the city's fame on social media, has resulted in overcrowding, environmental harm, and pressure on local resources (Simmons). The city's infrastructure, which is not built for such high numbers, is challenged, causing a reduction in the living standards for locals and a lesser experience for tourists (Simmons). Venice's struggles highlight the need for a balanced approach to technology and tourism, where the promotion and management of tourist influx are carefully calibrated to preserve the destination's integrity.

The examples of Singapore and Rwanda, set alongside the cautionary story of Venice, highlight the need for a thoughtful and balanced integration of technology in tourism. While technology can significantly enhance the visitor experience and aid conservation efforts, it is crucial to be aware of its potential to intensify issues like over-tourism. The lessons gleaned from these stories serve as a foundation upon which we can forecast emerging trends and developments likely to shape the trajectory of the tourism industry. Peering into the future of tourism, we can discern the outlines of several transformative trends driven by relentless technological innovation. These emerging patterns promise to redefine the traveler's experience and the industry's operations.

The rise of personalized travel is one such trend, where Artificial Intelligence and Big Data coalesce to offer tailor-made itineraries that resonate with individual preferences and past behaviors. Beyond customization, an imminent wave of automation and robotics is poised to streamline operations, from autonomous luggage handling at airports to robotic concierges in hotels. Emphasizing sustainability and integrating innovative technologies will be instrumental in lessening travel's ecological footprint.

Virtual reality (VR) and augmented reality (AR) are rapidly advancing, merging the digital and physical realms in unprecedented ways. These cutting-edge technologies stand at the brink of revolutionizing the pre-trip planning stages and on-site experiences at destinations, offering travelers novel and immersive ways to engage with different places.

The tourism industry's capacity for resilience and adaptation will face significant tests, requiring an active stance on innovation and agility in adapting to emerging challenges. In contemplating the future of tourism, we are not merely theorizing; we are preparing. By recognizing and understanding these evolving trends and forecasts, we are equipping ourselves for the unpredictable yet thrilling journey ahead. This ensures the tourism industry remains vibrant, responsive, and in tune with travelers' changing preferences and values worldwide.

Chapter 11

Unseen Battles and Debates: The Undercurrents of Tourism

The progression of tourism in the Northern Mariana Islands necessitates a comprehensive evaluation and comprehension of the associated difficulties and debates. Undeniably, tourism is a powerful economic catalyst, yet it harbors an unseen side. Each aspect of the tourism coin casts a light and a shadow; for the Northern Mariana Islands, this duality has ushered in complications ranging from environmental strain to cultural dilution and economic polarization.

The tension between elitist exclusivity and mass-market appeal in the Northern Mariana Islands sparks continuous debate, leaving a trail of economic disparity and cultural dilution. The pursuit of profit frequently clashes with the need for environmental stewardship, leading to a precarious balancing act that often favors short-term gains over long-term sustainability.

The silent socio-political dynamics that underpin these islands are fraught with complexity, often manifesting as invisible barriers that hinder genuine progress. The stark reality of these unseen battles raises uncomfortable questions about the future trajectory of tourism in the Northern Mariana Islands. Will the islands succumb to the pitfalls of over-commercialization, or will they find a way to navigate these turbulent waters?

As we journey through this chapter, we will confront the uncomfortable truths that cast a shadow over the tourism industry.

From the commodification of culture to the environmental degradation that threatens the islands' very existence, these are the battles that define the Northern Mariana Islands' struggle to preserve its soul amidst the relentless onslaught of tourism.

The tourism sector often caters to an elite clientele with the means to seek out high-end experiences. This practice usually favors a small group while overlooking the broader population. In contrast, the Northern Mariana Islands have historically focused on mass tourism. This approach is characterized by its openness to a wide array of visitors, eschewing the creation of exclusive, opulent areas in favor of more inclusive destinations. While this inclusivity makes travel experiences more accessible to a larger audience, it also comes with unique challenges that need addressing.

Mass tourism, while open to all, can lead to over-tourism, where the influx of visitors strains local infrastructure, depletes natural resources, and potentially undermines cultural authenticity. The Northern Mariana Islands experience these pressures, balancing the economic advantages of welcoming large numbers of tourists against the need to preserve their natural and cultural heritage.

These islands stand at a crucial point, navigating between the potential of catering to a wealthier clientele and the realities of a tourism model that prioritizes volume and accessibility. This situation mirrors a global debate in tourism: the allure of exclusivity versus the impact of mass accessibility. In the Northern Mariana Islands, this discussion unfolds nuancedly, carrying profound consequences for the future direction of tourism in this stunning archipelago.

While tourism brings economic benefits to the Northern Mariana Islands, it is essential to recognize the accompanying challenges. The islands gain financially from the influx of tourists.

However, they must also manage the less favorable impacts of this growth, striving to find a sustainable balance that honors their environment and community.

On one side, the influx of tourists translates into increased capital. Hotels, restaurants, and local attractions flourish, creating an illusion of a thriving economy. However, this prosperity is a paradox. The local businesses and industries that are the pillars of the islands' economy find themselves wrestling against a current of multinational chains and foreign investors who, attracted by the promise of profit, often overshadow the native enterprises.

Local artisans, shop owners, and service providers struggle to maintain their presence in a market increasingly dominated by foreign investors. As these international entities take root, the unique cultural identity of the islands is at risk of being diluted within a uniform commercial landscape, thereby eroding the very authenticity that once drew visitors from across the globe to its shores.

Furthermore, pursuing economic gain through tourism often contradicts sustainability principles. The Northern Mariana Islands face the daunting challenge of balancing the immediate appeal of financial profit against the long-term well-being of their natural and cultural resources. Infrastructure is under pressure from the growing demands, ecosystems weaken under the burden of development, and the cultural heritage is in danger of diluting in a flood of commercialization.

Thus, the economic impact of tourism is complex, where significant drawbacks check the benefits. In the Northern Mariana Islands, the challenge is not just harnessing the economic potential of tourism but doing so without compromising the islands' environmental integrity and cultural uniqueness. It is a nuanced balance that requires vision and dedication to sustainable development principles.

In the Northern Mariana Islands, the relentless march of tourism casts a long shadow over the once-vibrant cultural identity. The rich heritage and traditions, the lifeblood of its communities, now find themselves at a precarious juncture, threatened by the forces of commodification.

As the tourism industry expands, it inadvertently sidelines the culture it seeks to showcase. Local customs and ways of life are overshadowed by a culture tailored for tourists, with global entertainment and fast-food chains taking precedence over indigenous experiences. The unique cultural identity of the islands is at risk of being drowned out by a commercial landscape, diminishing the authenticity that once drew visitors to its shores.

Amidst this cultural shift, concerted efforts emerge to safeguard the islands' cultural heritage. Local activists, cultural practitioners, and concerned citizens are working towards safeguarding and maintaining the customs and traditions that define their identity. Initiatives aimed at cultural education and promoting authentic experiences strive to stem the tide of commodification. However, these endeavors often find themselves outmatched by the overwhelming force of a tourism industry more fixated on profit than preservation.

The struggle for cultural integrity in the Northern Mariana Islands is emblematic of a broader conflict, where the soul of a community contends with the commercial allure of tourism. As the islands grapple with this dilemma, the outcome of this unseen battle will shape the cultural landscape for generations to come.

The Northern Mariana Islands, a jewel of the Pacific, now confront the environmental consequences of unrestrained tourism.

The ecological impact of the industry, a testament to human oversight, grows increasingly significant.

The idyllic beaches, vibrant coral reefs, and lush tropical forests that once defined these islands face numerous threats. The arrival of tourists brings a deluge of waste, pollution, and ecological disruption, jeopardizing the islands' natural splendor. The once-crystal waters are now muddied with the detritus of human activity, and the coral reefs, those intricate underwater ecosystems, suffer from the impacts of climate change and irresponsible tourism.

Environmental degradation in the Northern Mariana Islands is not a hypothetical scenario but a current crisis. The relentless expansion of resorts and infrastructure encroaches on delicate habitats, disrupting the balance of the islands' ecosystems.

There are signs of resistance and resilience in the face of these challenges. Sustainable tourism practices are emerging to balance the islands' economic aspirations with ecological responsibility. Initiatives that promote environmentally friendly accommodations, effective waste management, and wildlife preservation are gaining traction, supported by a coalition of residents, environmental advocates, and progressive businesses.

Implementing these sustainable practices is challenging, facing obstacles from entrenched interests and limited resources. Nevertheless, these initiatives represent a crucial effort to counteract environmental neglect, which aims to safeguard the Northern Mariana Islands' natural legacy for future generations.

The current state of the islands marks a pivotal moment in the environmental crisis. The choices made today will determine the fate of their natural beauty - whether it will endure or fade into history. The situation of the Northern Mariana Islands highlights the fragility of our planet and underscores the urgent need for conscientious guardianship.

A storm brews in the socio-political realm in the shadow of the Northern Mariana Islands' picturesque landscapes. Tourism, a force of economic promise, has catalyzed deep-rooted political and social upheaval.

As resorts and hotels claim prime land, the local populace grapples with contentious land use, access, and ownership issues. These disputes are not merely legal squabbles; they are battles over the soul of the islands, pitting the relentless march of development against the sacredness of ancestral lands.

The burgeoning tourism industry has reshaped the social fabric of the islands, introducing a hierarchy skewed in favor of external investors and tourists. The local communities, once the stewards of the land, find themselves sidelined, their voices drowned out by the clamor of commerce. The development narrative is often scripted without their consent, leading to a sense of disempowerment and loss.

Activists and community leaders, refusing to be silent witnesses to this transformation, have risen to challenge the status quo. They advocate for equitable land policies, demand transparency in governance, and fight for the rights of indigenous populations. Their struggle is emblematic of a global phenomenon where the seductive promise of tourism revenue often eclipses the rights and dignity of local communities.

The intricate socio-political landscape of the Northern Mariana Islands mirrors a broader, more complex discussion challenging the core principles of contemporary tourism. This debate highlights a growing disparity: the contrast between those who profit from the tourism sector and those who shoulder its burdens. As the industry expands, this divide becomes increasingly pronounced.

Within these islands, simmering political tensions and the strain on social frameworks place the future of tourism under a microscope, sparking both keen interest and apprehension. Resolving these socio-political conflicts will be pivotal in shaping the islands' future, ultimately deciding if they can successfully navigate a course that respects their cultural legacy and future ambitions.

Technology emerges as a paradoxical force in the intricate conflicts that entangle the Northern Mariana Islands. Its swift advancement has stealthily permeated the tourism sector, becoming an unspoken contender in the ongoing disputes.

On one side, technology has leveled the playing field, offering unparalleled access to the islands' natural splendors. Every smartphone acts as a gateway, bringing the once-secluded corners of the Northern Marianas into the global spotlight. While this digital exposure boosts tourism, it also ignites fierce resource competition, intensifying the strained socio-political dynamics.

Nevertheless, these digital instruments that attract tourists also empower the local populace. Social media platforms magnify native voices, enabling them to project their stories to a worldwide audience. Technology has galvanized grassroots initiatives, challenging the entrenched power hierarchies that have long governed the islands' destiny.

However, this era of digital proliferation casts its shadows. The relentless chase for online presence and digital validation has led to the trivialization of culture, reducing sacred customs to mere tourist attractions. The genuineness of the islands risks being distorted through the lens of social media, altered to satisfy the visual demands of a digital audience.

The interaction between technology, accessibility, and sustainability in the Northern Mariana Islands is a nuanced ballet. Each advancement in digital innovation can either propel the islands towards a more just and sustainable future or pull them deeper into contention and deterioration. The role of technology in these unseen conflicts is crucial, and its influence, whether beneficial or detrimental, will resonate throughout the islands for years to come.

Peering into the uncertain future of the Northern Mariana Islands, the tourism sector finds itself at a critical juncture, its direction clouded by complex challenges and potential adversities. The path forward is not just a matter of statistics or economic forecasts; it is interwoven with various societal, environmental, and political factors, each vying for influence in the islands' destiny.

The years ahead will likely witness a continued rise in tourism, driven by a global populace constantly pursuing new experiences. The Northern Mariana Islands, with their unspoiled beaches and rich cultural tapestry, will remain a destination of choice. However, this increasing stream of visitors brings potential issues, threatening to strain the islands' resources and dilute the unique qualities that define them.

Discussions are heated as the islands confront the challenge of leveraging the economic benefits of tourism while preserving their natural and cultural assets. This delicate balance teeters on a knife-edge, with the shadow of over-commercialization ever-present. Initiatives to protect the islands' character face opposition, as the temptation of immediate profit often eclipses long-term sustainability goals.

Within this complex scenario, possible solutions begin to surface, though not without controversy. The enforcement of stricter regulations, encouraging eco-friendly tourism practices, and strengthening local communities emerge as promising paths forward. However, their adoption is met with resistance, as established interests and resistance to change pose formidable barriers.

The future of tourism in the Northern Mariana Islands remains unwritten; it is an evolving story shaped by present-day choices and actions. The undercurrent debates will mold this narrative, steering the islands toward a path that could culminate in either a robust, sustainable tourism sector or a missed opportunity and a squandered legacy. The deciding factors rest in the hands of influencers and those brave enough to challenge the established order, their voices resonating throughout the archipelago, influencing the shape of things to come.

A complex narrative has unfolded in the labyrinth of tourism's impact on the Northern Mariana Islands, marked by stark contrasts and profound questions. This chapter has traversed the dark underbelly of an industry often celebrated for its economic contributions, unearthing the contentious debates and unseen battles that simmer beneath the surface.

As the Northern Mariana Islands continue to navigate these turbulent waters, the role of stakeholders—government bodies, local communities, industry players, and environmental activists—becomes increasingly critical. Their collective actions, decisions, and compromises will not only shape the immediate trajectory of the tourism sector but also etch the long-term legacy of the islands themselves.

Navigating the way ahead is complex, fraught with potential pitfalls and unexpected outcomes. However, within this realm of uncertainty, there is a chance for meaningful conversation, creative solutions, and a fresh perspective on tourism that respects both the environment and the local community. The trajectory of tourism in the Northern Mariana Islands is at a critical juncture, and the outcome of this situation rests on the determination of influential figures equipped with strategic foresight and a profound commitment to the common good to tackle these issues courageously.

Chapter 12

Climate Change and Tourism: An Unavoidable Intersection

As we turn the pages to Chapter 12 of "Tourism Disrupted: How Elitism and Third-World Models Shape the Northern Mariana Islands," we must brace for the stark realities faced by the CNMI. Once the epitome of tourist allure with their pristine sands and lush underwater ecosystems, the islands now confront the relentless tide of climate upheaval. This once serene paradise, lauded for its natural wonders, stands on the precipice, staring down the dual threats of environmental degradation and a tourism industry in jeopardy.

The CNMI's picturesque beaches, a key draw for the tourism that sustains its economy, are succumbing to the voracious rise of the sea. Climate change, an ever-present aggressor, is not only claiming the islands' shores but also threatening to hollow out the marine sanctuaries that have long captivated divers and snorkelers from around the globe.

At the intersection of climate change and tourism, the CNMI's story unfolds as a cautionary tale of what happens when environmental stewardship is sidelined. The islands' struggle is a testament to the urgent need for action and adaptation, a reminder that the future of such paradises—and their economic lifelines—is contingent upon our global response to the climate crisis.

In the Northern Mariana Islands, climate change's physical and ecological impacts are no longer speculative concerns for a distant future; they are vivid and destructive realities of the present. The islands are not just changing; they are under siege by the forces of a changing climate.

The beaches of the CNMI, once expansive stretches of powdery white sand, are retreating under the relentless assault of rising sea levels. The erosion is not merely an aesthetic loss but a profound alteration of the islands' character and the foundation of their tourism appeal. Each inch of shore consumed by the ocean represents a tangible piece of the islands' heritage and economy that is washed away, a process silently swallowing up the landscapes that have been the backdrop to countless visitors' memories.

Under the ocean's surface, the situation is just as critical. Rising sea temperatures have caused extensive coral bleaching, robbing the reefs of their vivid hues and the myriad life forms they support (Maurin, 2020). These once-vibrant reefs are integral to the CNMI's marine-based tourism. Presently, they are reduced to ghostly remnants, stark indicators of the delicate condition of our aquatic ecosystems. This bleaching is more than an isolated occurrence; it is part of an alarming pattern indicating our ocean habitats' severe challenges.

Weather, previously a reliable aspect of tourism, has turned unpredictable and occasionally hostile in the CNMI. The islands are witnessing more intense and unexpected climatic events, from typhoons to extended heatwaves, disrupting tourism activities. These climatic shifts are problematic for visitors and the local infrastructure, potentially harming the islands' reputation as a desirable tourist locale in the long run.

The Pacific Islands Regional Climate Assessment report paints a grim picture of the future, with sea levels in the CNMI expected to rise by as much as 1.5 meters by the century's end (Grecni et al.,

2021). This is not a mere statistic but a potential death knell for the islands' geography as we know it. Such a rise would not only engulf large swathes of the beaches. However, it could also lead to the loss of both terrestrial and marine critical habitats, further jeopardizing the islands' biodiversity and attractiveness to nature-loving tourists.

The onslaught of climate change on the CNMI's delicate ecosystem is not just an ecological crisis but a dire threat to the tourism industry and these islands' economic lifeline. The damage being done is eroding the core attractions that have long defined the CNMI as a paradise for travelers.

Marine tourism, a pillar of the islands' allure, is in jeopardy as the ecological damage becomes increasingly apparent. Once vibrant and teeming with life, the coral reefs are bleaching to desolation. This bleaching—a stark indicator of stress caused by warmer ocean temperatures—renders the corals vulnerable to disease and death, disrupting the intricate web of marine life they support. For tourists, the appeal of diving into what were once underwater rainforests of biodiversity is waning, replaced by the disheartening sight of barren underwater landscapes. The impact extends beyond the disappointment of tourists; it affects the livelihoods of local dive operators, fishermen, and other stakeholders who rely on a healthy marine ecosystem for their income.

The unpredictable weather patterns further compound the islands' woes. Where tourists once could bank on the reliability of the CNMI's tropical climate, they now face the uncertainty of travel disruptions and safety concerns. The increasing frequency and intensity of typhoons are not merely inconveniences but natural hazards. The destruction left in the wake of such storms can devastate infrastructure and deter potential visitors, casting a shadow of doubt over the islands' image as a serene and secure destination.

This erratic weather also has subtler but no less significant consequences. Extended periods of unexpected heat or rain can disrupt the peak tourist seasons, leading to a decline in visitor numbers and a hit to the tourism-dependent economy. Such fluctuations can turn the once bustling beaches and resorts into stretches of unpeopled sand and empty rooms, signaling a troubling downturn for the industry.

The reality is that the CNMI's status as a tourist haven is at stake. The changing climate is reshaping the islands into a place of unpredictability and loss, a far cry from the idyllic escape promised in travel brochures. As the natural attractions suffer, so too does the very essence of what draws people to these distant shores—the guarantee of an untouched, stable, and welcoming paradise.

The challenge is immense, and the stakes are high. The CNMI must navigate these turbulent waters, finding ways to adapt and preserve what remains of its natural heritage or risk watching its main economic driver—the tourism industry—flounder in the face of climate change's relentless tide.

In a world where climate change is not just knocking at the door but has already invited itself in, the tourism industry in the CNMI faces a stark reality. It must reckon with its role in this environmental upheaval and recognize that traditional tourism models are unsustainable in the face of such ecological adversity.

The CNMI's tourism sector finds itself at a critical juncture, where continuing on the current path is tantamount to contributing to its demise. Sustainable practices are no longer commendable choices; they are essential strategies for survival. The idyllic images sold to tourists are under threat from the very footprint left by their visits. If the industry fails to adapt, it risks exacerbating the environmental crisis and losing the natural heritage it relies on for economic prosperity.

Eco-tourism, often touted as a win-win for conservation and local communities, must be more than a token gesture in the CNMI. It demands a robust and sincere commitment that goes beyond the superficial. Tourists participating in conservation efforts must do so with the understanding that their actions are a drop in the ocean of what is required to combat the more significant issue. While beneficial, planting a few corals or removing invasive species does not offset the broader impacts of global travel and the carbon emissions it generates.

The environmental initiatives touted by the tourism industry warrant a closer, more critical examination. While implementing solar panels and energy-efficient appliances marks a positive beginning, these measures represent a modest advance in the extensive journey toward true environmental sustainability. Similarly, the emphasis on local food sourcing is commendable, but it should be part of a broader strategy to significantly reduce the tourism sector's overall carbon footprint.

Transitioning to sustainable practices presents several challenges, including the financial costs and potential opposition from those who benefit from the current system. However, the alternative — a tourism industry that exhausts the resources it depends on — is a short-sighted and counterproductive approach.

Thus, as the CNMI grapples with the relentless progression of climate change, its tourism industry must adopt a more sustainable model not as a marketing strategy but as a necessary evolution. Doing so may preserve the environment and the cultural and economic fabric that depends so heavily upon it. Anything less would be a disservice to future generations who might only experience the CNMI's once-pristine beauty through stories and old photographs.

The grim reality for the CNMI's tourism sector is that more than incremental changes and half-measures in sustainability are needed. The industry is confronted with the urgent need to overhaul its environmental footprint—a daunting task that requires decisive action rather than tentative steps.

Renewable energy, often touted as a beacon of hope, remains glaringly underutilized within the CNMI's tourism operations. The islands bask in the sunlight and are caressed by winds that could easily be harnessed to power the establishments that play host to the world. Nevertheless, inertia and short-term financial concerns have stymied the widespread adoption of solar panels and wind turbines, which could dramatically cut reliance on expensive, imported fossil fuels.

The culinary experience in the CNMI, while rich in flavors, often overlooks the heavy carbon toll of importing food. There is a dire need to pivot towards local produce and seafood, which could carve a path for a more authentic and environmentally conscious dining experience. This shift would cut down on the carbon emissions from shipping and pour much-needed financial support into local communities, fostering a more resilient local economy.

Waste management is another critical issue the tourism sector must address more effectively. Despite the glaring need for robust recycling programs and the reduction of plastic waste, progress has been tepid. The consequences of such negligence are etched into the landscape—littered beaches, polluted waters, and a natural beauty under siege.

The concept of conservation is often given lip service, but implementing a culture that genuinely reflects these values is rare. Tourist facilities must move beyond mere signage asking guests to reuse towels and embed sustainability into the very fabric of the visitor experience. Guests should be immersed in an environment that encourages and necessitates participation in conservation efforts.

The harsh truth is that achieving sustainability in the CNMI's tourism industry is fraught with financial, cultural, and logistical hurdles. Nevertheless, the price of not taking action is even greater. Failing to pivot towards sustainable practices endangers the industry by contributing to the degradation of the environment it depends upon. Immediate, impactful action is crucial; the fate of the CNMI's natural beauty and tourism sector is at a critical point.

In a climate increasingly hostile to the fragile equilibriums of island ecosystems, the Northern Mariana Islands are confronted with a harsh truth: their infrastructure, the backbone of the tourism industry, is at the mercy of a tempestuous environment. The call to action for climate-resilient construction is not just another box to check—it is an urgent plea to fend off the inevitable onslaught that climate change brings.

The current landscape of tourism infrastructure in the CNMI is precariously perched on the edge of a climate cliff. Traditional structures and facilities are vulnerable, awaiting the next super typhoon or the inexorable rise of the ocean to claim them. The need for storm-resistant architecture is no longer a future consideration but a present-day imperative. Without it, the islands could see their primary source of income—and the livelihoods that depend on it—washed away or blown apart, perhaps never to be reclaimed.

Beach erosion, that slow-motion disaster, is not just washing away grains of sand; it is eroding the very identity of the islands as a slice of tropical heaven. Countermeasures, like the construction of artificial reefs, are an essential defense. These reefs double as conservation efforts, serving the dual purpose of shoreline protection and marine biodiversity enhancement, essential to luring the eco-aware traveler.

There is also a pressing need to overhaul the islands' emergency response systems. Advanced early warning mechanisms are critical, not just for protecting life and property but as a statement of preparedness that can reassure jittery tourists contemplating a visit to this increasingly vulnerable paradise.

The CNMI's tourism sector must pivot towards a future where sustainability is not just a buzzword but a foundational principle of every new development. This calls for a formidable investment in durable, climate-conscious infrastructure that may seem overwhelming in the face of limited resources and immediate economic pressures. Nevertheless, this transition is the only path forward for a tourism industry that aims to survive, let alone thrive, in an age where the rules written by nature are becoming ever more stringent and unforgiving.

As the CNMI faces an escalating battle against the forces of climate change, the tourism sector holds a double-edged sword. On one side is the unquenchable thirst for exotic vacations in pristine environments; on the other, there is a creeping awareness that these desires fuel the environmental degradation they seek to escape. In this precarious balance, educating tourists about climate change becomes not merely beneficial but critical.

Ignorance in this context is far from bliss. It is a malignant force, driving unsustainable practices that contribute to the degradation of the very attractions that tourists come to experience. Educating those who visit the CNMI about the intricate and often invisible threads that connect their presence to the islands' health is a responsibility the tourism industry can no longer afford to sidestep. It is about transforming tourists from passive consumers into informed, responsible travelers who understand the weight of their footprints on the delicate sands of these island shores.

The task is to integrate climate change education into every aspect of the tourist experience, from the moment of arrival to the final farewell. It is about infusing knowledge into guided tours, integrating sustainable practices into every hotel stay, and ensuring that each dive into the ocean is also a dive into understanding the fragile marine ecosystems. This education can take shape through interactive workshops, informational displays at key natural sites, or partnerships with conservation organizations.

Educating tourists goes beyond just sharing knowledge; it is about nurturing a culture of care and shared responsibility. It is about instilling that while these islands offer relaxation and rejuvenation, they also demand respect and protection. The ultimate aim is to cultivate a group of visitors who depart from the CNMI with memories and keepsakes, a deepened awareness of their part in the global ecosystem, and a dedication to being ambassadors of sustainability.

As the climate emergency intensifies, the urgency for this type of education grows. The CNMI has a chance to set a precedent, demonstrating that tourism can be more than just a passive participant in environmental decline; it can actively contribute to preserving natural beauty and biodiversity. By doing so, the islands enhance the visitor experience and ensure that the charm that attracts tourists to their shores endures for future generations.

The CNMI is confronting a critical reality defined by climate change. This new reality threatens the very pillars of its tourism sector, with rising sea levels, devastated coral reefs, and severe storms. These challenges are not mere disruptions; they foretell a bleak future where the CNMI's idyllic landscapes, once central to its economic prosperity, face the risk of fading into history.

The challenges before the CNMI are immense, casting long shadows over a paradise that once seemed untouchable. The islands face the prospect of watching their natural wonders, once a lure for travelers from across the globe, become tarnished by the relentless march of environmental degradation. However, within this brewing storm lies a sliver of opportunity for the CNMI to pivot, harness the moment's urgency, and turn the tide.

The tourism industry, now at the mercy of the elements it has taken for granted, must rise to an unprecedented occasion. The path forward is fraught with difficulties that demand bold, innovative responses. This is a call to action for the CNMI to redefine the essence of travel in the age of climate awareness to move beyond the short-sighted pursuits of profit at the expense of sustainability.

In this crucial period, the tourism sector of the CNMI stands at a crossroads. The choice is stark: watch passively as environmental shifts undermine the economic base or proactively reorganize and align with nature. This juncture offers a chance to demonstrate globally how tourism can transform from an exclusive luxury into a sustainable and inclusive festivity, safeguarding the CNMI's natural wonders for future generations.

However, time is of the essence, and the opportunity for meaningful action is diminishing. Whether the CNMI will respond to this urgent call or stand by as its beaches, economy, and essence are gradually eroded. The steps taken now, or their absence, will either affirm the islands' commitment to change or stand as a mournful testament to a paradise lost to the escalating challenges of climate change. The story of the CNMI's future remains to be written, and it lies in the hands of those ready to confront today's challenges to secure a more sustainable tomorrow.

As this exploration of the Northern Mariana Islands and the ominous shadow of climate change draws to a close, we are left to contemplate a sobering conclusion. Once the bedrock of its tourism appeal, the stark transformation of the CNMI's natural landscapes is no longer a distant possibility but an unfolding reality. This is not a scenario we can afford to meet with complacency; instead, it requires an immediate, robust response that intertwines the very survival of the tourism industry with proactive climate change mitigation strategies.

The CNMI's future, much like that of many idyllic destinations around the globe, hangs in a delicate balance. The islands' once-thriving tourist hubs face the threat of becoming silent witnesses to the relentless rise of the oceans, the bleaching of coral reefs, and the unpredictable fury of nature's altered patterns. This wake-up call rings with urgency for a collective global responsibility—a call to preserve the natural beauty of places like the CNMI for posterity and ensure their economic vitality remains intact.

The tourism industry, which has long reaped the rewards of the CNMI's natural splendor, must now adopt and advocate for sustainable practices beyond mere tokenism. It is incumbent upon those who benefit from the world's natural havens to invest in their preservation. This means rethinking development models, embracing renewable energies, reducing waste, and educating every traveler about their role in harming or healing the places they visit.

At this point, the choices we make will echo across future generations. Merely admiring nature's beauty is no longer sufficient; we must actively protect it. The CNMI and destinations worldwide need a fresh approach where tourism and environmental protection are not adversaries but partners in building a sustainable future.

The CNMI's story reflects a broader, global challenge, urging all tourism stakeholders to adopt a new mindset. This is a plea to safeguard our planet's intricate fabric, forging a response as widespread as the effects of climate change. For the CNMI and other vulnerable locales worldwide, we must respond with determination, solidarity, and the awareness that our actions today will shape their future.

Chapter 13

Policy and Governance: Steering the Course of Tourism Development in the CNMI

Northern Mariana Islands probes the intricate relationship between policy, governance, and the future direction of tourism in the CNMI. The islands, known for their pristine beauty and rich culture, are now faced with critical decisions that will shape the sustainability of their tourism sector. In the CNMI, the once-celebrated tourism sector now faces a reckoning with the consequences of its growth. The strategies and regulatory frameworks enacted to cultivate a thriving tourism economy are due for a stern reassessment, as they have set the islands on a precarious path.

The governance of tourism here has its contradictions. It is a juggling act of enforcing sustainable measures against a relentless push for expansion and profits. This push and pull starkly reflects the broader struggle between exploiting nature for economic gain and the urgent need to preserve it. The islands are caught in a discordant dance, luring visitors with promises of untouched beauty while simultaneously laying the groundwork for its potential spoiling. Policies once seen as the engines of prosperity now risk becoming agents of destruction, threatening the essence of the CNMI's appeal.

The chapter ahead explores these dissonances, a critique of the CNMI's approach to managing its golden goose of tourism. It accounts for short-sighted ambitions clashing with the imperative of enduring conservation of a community's culture and environment caught in the crossfire of governance and the relentless pursuit of economic gains. The nascent phase of the CNMI's tourism industry was a time of unbridled optimism. Developers and policymakers alike saw the islands' breathtaking vistas and strategic location as a veritable gold mine for tourism. The government, eager to capitalize on this potential, rolled out the red carpet for investors, offering generous tax breaks and mitigating regulatory hurdles. In this heady era, the environmental and cultural treasures of the CNMI were relegated to mere backdrops for tourist activities, with little thought given to their preservation. As the industry burgeoned, it brought an economic vitality that was hard to ignore. The rush to build and capitalize on the islands' allure often proceeded with scant regard for the long-term implications. Resorts, golf courses, and attractions sprang up, altering the islands' landscape and socio-cultural fabric in irreversible ways.

Governance, too, transformed the reins of power and changed hands. Each new administration brought its vision for the future of tourism, sometimes pivoting towards sustainability, at other times favoring aggressive expansion. The policies that emerged from these shifts were mixed; some fostered a sense of stewardship over the islands' natural resources, while others continued to champion unfettered growth. A retrospective gaze at these policy initiatives reveals a pattern of hits and misses. There seemed to be a stumble for every stride taken towards protecting marine habitats or supporting local traditions. This initiative faltered due to poor execution or opposition from powerful interests rooted in the status quo. The well-being of the islands often took a back seat to the allure of quick profits and the relentless drumbeat of expansion.

This historical panorama of policy-making in the CNMI serves as a cautionary tale. It shows that good intentions are not enough;

policies must be informed by a deep understanding of the local context and backed by the will to see them through. The islands have seen what happens when short-term gains are prioritized over the sustainable use of their precious natural and cultural assets. As they move forward, the painful lessons of the past must inform a more cautious and conscientious approach to tourism policy—one that respects the delicate balance between economic vigor and the imperative to preserve the CNMI's irreplaceable treasures for future generations.

The current tourism policy environment in the CNMI has been shaped with the dual intentions of stimulating economic growth and preserving the environmental and cultural assets that define the islands. These policies range from incentivizing foreign investment to stringent measures to safeguard the archipelago's natural wonders and cultural heritage. Their efficacy, however, remains a topic of heated debate, with criticisms focusing on their adequacy in protecting local interests or, conversely, their potential to hinder economic progress.

The CNMI government's role in tourism development has traditionally been an active promoter, striving to foster a welcoming atmosphere for tourists and investors. This stance is increasingly being questioned, as there is a call for a shift towards a model that balances economic growth with sustainable practices and the long-term preservation of ecological and cultural integrity. The government's initiatives and partnerships, particularly concerning tourism, are scrutinized for their true alignment with the sustainable development goals often touted in official rhetoric.

The regulatory oversight of tourism falls to various bodies, each tasked with specific aspects of tourism management. From environmental protection agencies to cultural preservation offices, these bodies ensure that the tourism sector operates within a framework that protects the islands' interests. However, these agencies often face limited resources, bureaucratic delays, and sometimes conflicting mandates, which can impede their ability to effectively manage a sector that is both an economic lifeline and a potential threat to the islands' sustainability.

The economic strategies that aim to boost the CNMI's tourism growth carry inherent risks. For example, tax incentives might attract investors, catalyze growth, and siphon off potential revenue from environmental conservation efforts. These financial gambits are risky; they offer temporary boosts at the expense of long-term economic health. In addition, the CNMI's dependence on foreign workers in the tourism sector points to broader economic vulnerabilities within the local job market. Labor regulations often inadequately protect the rights of these workers, creating an exploited workforce propping up the industry. This reliance undermines local employment opportunities and leaves the islands at the mercy of international labor trends and policy changes. Also, financial support for tourism businesses usually comes after crises, serving as emergency aid rather than a strategic foundation for stability. This approach fails to address the underlying vulnerabilities of an economy heavily dependent on the unpredictable nature of global tourism. Overall, the economic policies related to tourism in the CNMI tend to prioritize quick fixes over sustainable practices. These policies contribute to a fragile economic state, prioritizing short-term gains over the stability and sustainability needed for long-term economic health and environmental preservation.

The CNMI's environmental policies are designed to safeguard its priceless ecosystems, the backbone of the island's tourism allure. These policies, while well-intentioned, often grapple with the harsh realities of enforcement and the relentless drive for economic progress. A slew of regulations exist to protect the CNMI's diverse habitats. However, these are consistently put to the test by a tourism sector that has been too willing to place revenue above environmental health. The tension between economic development and ecological sustainability is palpable, as the islands' lush landscapes and vibrant marine life are caught in the crosshairs of competing interests. Sustainable development remains a core objective on the legislative agenda, but the transition from policy to action is fraught with obstacles. *Enforcement* is an uphill battle, hampered by limited resources and the temptation to overlook long-term environmental consequences for immediate financial gain.

The reality of policy enforcement in the CNMI is a patchwork of successes and failures. On the one hand, there are inspiring success stories where enforcement has turned the tide, safeguarding habitats and helping endangered species to flourish. On the other, there are stark warnings — tales of oversight and neglect, where delicate ecosystems have been compromised, sometimes irreversibly, by the pressures of unbridled tourism and haphazard development. By confronting the shortcomings and celebrating the wins, the CNMI can glean valuable insights into the complex dance of protecting natural beauty while fostering a thriving tourism sector. This balance remains elusive but increasingly necessary. The CNMI ecosystem and cultural heritage are compromised.

The CNMI's cultural heritage, a mosaic rich with tradition, history, and an indigenous identity that has endured centuries of change, now faces the complex task of weaving these elements into the fabric of its tourism industry. As the islands continue attracting visitors, the policies safeguarding this heritage are tasked with integrating cultural authenticity into a sector frequently dominated by superficial consumer trends.

Central to these policies is the dedication to honoring and sharing the unique Chamorro and Carolinian cultures. Initiatives to enrich the tourism experience with genuine local customs and traditions go beyond mere cultural exhibitionism; they also distinguish the CNMI's tourism offerings from other destinations. Nonetheless, navigating the fine line between showcasing culture for educational purposes and commodifying it for entertainment is a nuanced operation.

These endeavors, which include cultural festivals, artisan markets, historic site preservation, and museum exhibits, aim to provide tourists with an enriching encounter with the CNMI's cultural spirit while supporting local communities' economic fabric. The challenge, however, lies in ensuring these cultural expressions remain genuine and not overly tailored or altered for tourist appeal.

Finding a balance between maintaining cultural authenticity and capitalizing on its economic potential is akin to walking a fine line. It requires policies sensitive to cultural values designed to empower rather than exploit. The CNMI's strategy in this respect is pivotal; it must foster a tourism industry that respects tradition, engages with the present-day cultural landscape, and ensures that the deep-seated cultural narratives are preserved for the enjoyment and education of future generations. However, the CNMI is in dire need of new culture-related policies and infrastructure policies.

The current state of the CNMI's tourism infrastructure is at a crossroads between necessary growth and the urgent call for sustainability. The islands' transportation, beset with outdated facilities, needs a comprehensive revamp to manage the influx of tourists while also considering the environmental toll. The lack of foresight in policy-making has resulted in stopgap solutions that fail to address the long-term needs of sustainable mobility. In addition, Utilities, the lifeblood of tourism operations, are plagued by decay and inefficiency. Hotels and restaurants grapple with unreliable power and water supply, which tarnishes the visitor experience and reflects a deeper negligence in policy planning. Despite the apparent need for investment in modern and sustainable utility systems, policymakers have been content with piecemeal repairs that are woefully inadequate. Also, in the accommodation sector, the rush to expand lodging capacity is outpacing the consideration for ecological impact. The result is a haphazard property development that consumes landscapes and strains local ecosystems. Environmental policies that could guide responsible growth appear to be an afterthought, overshadowed by the pressing drive for economic returns. The current policies reveal a pattern of disregard for the long-term health of the islands in favor of short-term economic interests—a risky gamble with the islands' future at stake.

In the CNMI, the interplay between nature's unpredictability and human preparedness is starkly evident. The region's vulnerability to natural disasters, such as typhoons and global crises like pandemics, has repeatedly put its tourism policies to the test.

Disaster preparedness within the tourism sector has historically been reactive rather than proactive, with the islands often scrambling to respond in the aftermath of a crisis. While the government has established emergency protocols, their execution during critical moments has exposed significant gaps. The lack of comprehensive strategies specific to the needs of the tourism industry, including tourists themselves, local businesses, and the workforce, has resulted in chaotic responses that exacerbate the impact of crises.

Policies intended to manage tourism during such disruptive events have suffered from a lack of clarity and coordination. For instance, the communication breakdown between government agencies and tourism operators often leads to conflicting information and a disjointed recovery effort. This confusion not only hampers immediate relief efforts but also has a long-lasting effect on the islands' reputation as a safe and reliable destination.

The CNMI's experiences with past crises, including devastating typhoons and the global COVID-19 pandemic, have laid bare the shortcomings in crisis management. Each event has been a learning experience, highlighting the need for robust contingency planning, resource allocation, and stakeholder engagement. The aftermath has often seen a surge in discussions and planning sessions aimed at bolstering tourism resilience, yet the implementation of such plans remains inconsistent.

As the islands grapple with the lessons from these events, a critical examination of past responses is necessary. This reflection must translate into tangible policy enhancements that prioritize the safety of both visitors and residents. Moreover, it is imperative to build a culture of preparedness that permeates the entire tourism ecosystem, ensuring that when the next crisis strikes, the CNMI is not caught off-guard but is equipped to manage and mitigate the repercussions effectively.

Tourism policy in the Northern Mariana Islands has long been the domain of the few, often sidelining those who bear the consequences of its outcomes: the local communities. Their marginalization from policy discussions is more than just a procedural oversight; it fails to recognize the human dimension of tourism's footprint. The islands' tourism narrative is incomplete without the chapters written by people whose heritage and daily realities are tourist attractions.

Non-Governmental Organizations (NGOs) have been vocal in this space, advocating for a more equitable approach to tourism development. They argue against the myopic visions of a tourism strategy that prizes immediate profits over long-term communal and environmental health. While noble, their campaigns and policy suggestions often clash with the government and private sector's economic imperatives. This creates a tug-of-war that leaves policies hanging in the balance, skewed by the heavier weight of capital interests.

Private sector influence in policy-making is unmistakable. With tourism being a significant economic driver for the CNMI, businesses have a substantial stake in policy outcomes. However, their involvement raises questions about whose interests are being served. Are these policies sculpting a landscape that treasures the CNMI's unique cultural tapestry and natural beauty, or are they carving out greater profits at the expense of the islands' soul?

The current state of stakeholder participation in the CNMI's tourism policy-making is often overlooked, and business interests have a disproportionate sway. It is time to call for a more adversarial but necessary shift towards a governance model that does not just pay lip service to collaboration but enshrines it, even if it means confronting the uncomfortable truth that the tourism industry's gains have been unequally shared and its costs unevenly distributed.

The CNMI can draw practical lessons from various islands that have harmoniously blended their tourism industries with environmental and cultural preservation.

Iceland has adeptly managed a recent visitor surge, leveraging its natural wonders to boost the economy while enforcing rigorous environmental safeguards (2021). These measures ensure that its dramatic landscapes remain unspoiled for future generations.

Fiji presents a model where tourism directly benefits local people, ensuring that cultural practices and the community's well-being are at the forefront of tourist interactions, providing a more authentic and equitable tourism model (2023).

The Azores have focused on eco-tourism, where a commitment to environmental preservation matches the allure of volcanic landscapes and lush greenery (2022). This shows that tourism need not be at odds with nature.

The Galápagos Islands exemplify the benefits of stringent visitor management and a focus on conservation, preserving the archipelago's unique biodiversity and serving as a living laboratory for evolutionary studies (Rosenfeld, 2023).

When the tourism policies of the CNMI are held up against the light of other island destinations, the comparison reveals a stark disparity. Many island nations have carved out tourism niches that bolster their economies and safeguard their environments and cultures. The CNMI's approach often appears myopic in this global context, prioritizing rapid economic gains over preserving its irreplaceable natural and cultural assets. Although no model can be transplanted without adaptation, the principles of successful island tourism policies are universal and can illuminate the path forward for the CNMI.

In the realm of CNMI's tourism, there is a persistent struggle to bring lofty policy declarations down to the gritty reality of everyday life. Political forces often treat tourism policy as a game of musical chairs, hastily altering strategies with each change in administration, leaving long-term planning by the wayside. Such a haphazard approach breeds inconsistency, undermining any chance of meaningful progress.

Economically, the islands are perched on a shaky foundation, their fortunes too closely tied to the whims of the global tourist market. Policy responses are often reactive when the economic winds shift, aiming for quick fixes that seldom address deeper systemic issues. This short-sightedness is evident in the over-reliance on foreign workers, which only highlights the failure to cultivate a robust local workforce, leaving the economy in a perpetual state of imbalance.

Social barriers further widen the chasm between policy and implementation. There is an undeniable rift between the policymakers ensconced in their offices and the local communities most impacted by these decisions. Policies hatched in isolation seldom take root, facing pushback from those whose interests and insights are ignored, rendering such policies ineffective.

CNMI needs to rethink its approach to tackle these entrenched issues radically. It is not just about drafting policies but also about fostering resilience against the whims of political change, investing in the local people to reduce reliance on imported labor, and genuinely listening to the islanders' voices. Can the CNMI only hope to craft tourism policies that look good on paper and bring tangible benefits to its lands and people by addressing these core challenges?

The CNMI's future tourism strategies need to confront harsh realities. The islands must transcend short-term economic boosts and instead engrain sustainability into the tourism ethos, with an eye on preserving its environmental and cultural legacies. To avoid the pitfalls of unpreparedness and ensure a resilient future for its tourism industry, the CNMI should consider urgent, concrete steps:

Disincentivize Unsustainability: Implement a punitive framework for businesses that neglect environmental standards, counterbalancing enticements for sustainable practices.

Mandate Community Profit-Sharing: Enforce regulations that ensure tourism profits feed back into local communities, maintaining cultural dignity and social equity.

Require Sustainability Training: Allocate funds strictly for education programs focused on sustainable tourism, creating a homegrown workforce prepared for tomorrow's industry standards.

Insist on Climate-Proof Infrastructure: Channel investments into building and retrofitting structures to endure climate disruptions to avoid the extreme post-disaster rebuilding costs.

Demand Technological Integration: Introduce mandates for the tourism industry to incorporate advanced technologies for improving visitor experiences and resource management.

Implement a Strict Monitoring Regime: Establish unyielding monitoring of tourism trends and policy outcomes, with swift penalties for policy breaches to enforce compliance.

Enforce Collaborative Governance: Press for a governance model that does not merely suggest but requires cross-sector collaboration for a comprehensive approach to tourism.

By taking these steps, the CNMI can do more than salvage its tourism industry—it can forge a new path that aligns economic ambition with the imperative to protect its natural beauty and cultural identity. It is a challenging journey, marked by potential resistance and the need for unwavering commitment. However, it is also the CNMI's best chance at maintaining its status as a sought-after destination.

The CNMI must embrace a dynamic, inclusive, and forward-thinking governance model. Policymakers, stakeholders, and the community must unite to ensure that tourism policies are well-crafted and resonate with the aspirations of the people they affect. It is not enough to draft policy; there must be a concerted effort to breathe life into these regulations, transforming them into tangible actions that safeguard the CNMI's tourism industry for generations.

This is a call to action to protect, preserve, and prosper within the bounds of our natural world and cultural heritage.

Chapter 14

Social Impact of Diverse Tourism Types

The Northern Mariana Islands, a destination renowned for its diverse tourism opportunities, presents a picture-perfect postcard to the world. However, a more complex narrative exists beyond the serene beaches and lush landscapes that profoundly affect the local populace. It reflects the contrast between the vibrant images sold to tourists and the less-visible realities the islanders live with—realities that sometimes include hardship and cultural compromise. This chapter aims to unravel the complex layers of the CNMI's tourism sector, raising essential questions about the societal effects of each type of tourism. How does each type of tourism shape the social landscape? At what cost and how does each tourism model influence the social framework?

Mass Tourism and Its Social Consequences

Mass tourism's arrival to the Northern Mariana Islands has been both a boon and a bane. The allure of sun-soaked beaches and the promise of relaxation draw countless visitors, providing a significant thrust to the local economy. The financial infusion from this type of tourism can be seen in the bustling markets, the livelihoods it supports, and the infrastructure it builds. However, this influx has its complex social consequences.

One of the most pronounced drawbacks is the cultural dilution that often accompanies the waves of tourists. The need to cater to a global audience can lead to the commodification of local traditions, as cultural performances and artifacts are repackaged for mass consumption. This distorts the authenticity of the cultural experience and risks reducing deeply meaningful practices to mere spectacles for entertainment.

As the islands accommodate a growing number of visitors, the strain on infrastructure and resources becomes increasingly apparent. Once quiet roads are now trafficked by tour buses and car rentals, and beaches that offered solace to locals are now crowded with tourists. The surge in demand often outpaces the capacity of local utilities, leading to issues like water shortages and power outages, which disproportionately affect the resident population.

The repercussions of extensive tourism on the environment are significant. There is a notable rise in waste production, a heavy burden on natural resources, and an increased likelihood of environmental damage due to unchecked development. These challenges present long-term severe threats to the ecological health of the islands, which is essential for the well-being of residents and for maintaining the charm of these destinations for tourists.

The social landscape also contends with an economy pivoting heavily on the tourism sector, making the local communities vulnerable to the ebbs and flows of global travel trends. A downturn in tourist numbers, whether due to economic recessions, natural disasters, or pandemics, can lead to significant economic hardship for those whose livelihoods depend on visitor spending.

The CNMI must carefully consider the long-term ramifications of courting mass tourism. While the economic allure is tempting, weighing such benefits against potential cultural and environmental costs is crucial. A prudent approach would involve planning and community engagement to ensure that the islands' unique heritage and natural resources are not compromised for transient economic gains.

Ecotourism and Community Engagement

Ecotourism is a promising path for the Northern Mariana Islands, charting a course that balances economic activity with preserving its pristine environments. It departs from the more aggressive tourism models, advocating for a lighter footprint where economic progress does not necessitate environmental degradation or cultural erosion. In the CNMI, ecotourism is beginning to shape an economic narrative that places community enrichment and the guardianship of nature at its heart.

This responsible approach to travel centered around natural areas aims to uphold environmental conservation while enhancing local livelihoods. The CNMI's endeavors in ecotourism should actively engage residents, including those who work the land, create with their hands, and run local enterprises, directly into the tourism industry's fabric. From showcasing native crops in farm-to-table initiatives to providing a platform for selling locally made crafts, ecotourism's main objective is weaving the islands' cultural and agricultural threads into the tourist experience.

Effective ecotourism relies heavily on the meaningful inclusion of the community. It is not merely about token participation; it requires honoring local insight and addressing community-specific needs. It is about establishing channels for local perspectives to influence and direct the trajectory of tourism development, ensuring it resonates with the residents' vision for their homeland.

Besides fostering economic opportunities, ecotourism is an educational conduit for island visitors and inhabitants. Activities like interpretative trails and conservation projects impart a greater understanding and respect for the CNMI's unique ecosystems.

Visitors leave with a heightened environmental consciousness, while residents are bolstered as custodians of their natural legacy.

The community's involvement in ecotourism transcends mere business interactions; it is about building an authentic partnership that recognizes and elevates the voices of the local populace, especially those whose livelihoods have traditionally been intertwined with the natural environment. Policy frameworks must be crafted with inclusivity at their core, ensuring that the dividends of ecotourism are distributed equitably and that initiatives evolve in concert with local desires and objectives.

Nevertheless, the path of ecotourism is strewn with challenges. As it scales, maintaining the integrity of its sustainable tenets is paramount. Vigilance is necessary to prevent the dilution of its core values and to guard against the guise of greenwashing.

For the CNMI, fully embracing ecotourism offers the prospect of redefining its tourism narrative. It presents an opportunity to integrate indigenous agricultural practices, protect natural habitats, and foster genuine community involvement. Ecotourism is not just about safeguarding scenic landscapes—it is about reinforcing the socioeconomic foundation of the island's communities and ensuring a harmonious and enduring symbiosis between the land and its stewards.

Cultural Tourism: Preservation or Commodification?

Cultural tourism in the Northern Mariana Islands treads a delicate line between showcasing the rich heritage of the islands and the potential commodification of its traditions. This form of tourism offers visitors an immersive experience of the islands' history, art, and customs, potentially fostering a deep appreciation and respect for the local culture. It stands as an interactive museum, a living narrative that invites tourists to step into the story of the CNMI.

Cultural tourism, at its most effective, is a vital means of preservation. It offers the financial resources necessary for restoring historical landmarks, aiding local artisans, and keeping traditional customs that might otherwise disappear. This form of tourism allows island residents to embrace and celebrate their heritage, ensuring its survival for future generations.

Conversely, the blend of culture and commerce can commodify cultural aspects. When cultural traditions are modified to suit tourist tastes, there is a danger of trivializing what is sacred and historically important, turning them into simple attractions. This situation prompts critical questions about the authenticity and true representation of cultural practices. It begs the question: Are visitors experiencing the authentic culture of the CNMI or just a polished, commercially viable version?

One of the core concerns is ensuring that the portrayal of local culture is accurate and respectful. It involves a dialogue with the community to decide how their culture is presented and shared. In the CNMI, this means engaging with local historians, cultural practitioners, and the broader community to create tourism experiences that are authentic and mutually beneficial.

Moreover, the focus should be on sustainable cultural tourism, where the benefits are distributed fairly among the community members. This requires policies prioritizing local empowerment over profit, ensuring that external interests do not hijack the cultural narrative.

The challenge is to manage cultural tourism so that it does not overwhelm or distort local culture but instead supports and amplifies it. It should not lead to a homogenized version of culture that caters to what is assumed to be the tourists' tastes. Instead, it should accurately reflect the CNMI's traditions, telling the stories of its people through their voices and perspectives.

In the Northern Mariana Islands, the potential of cultural tourism is vast. It can contribute to a sense of identity and community pride while providing educational value to visitors. The key is to pursue this form of tourism with a conscientious approach that prioritizes cultural integrity and empowerment. By doing so, the CNMI can ensure that cultural tourism contributes positively to the social fabric of the islands, preserving its unique cultural landscape for future generations.

Adventure Tourism and Risk Management

The thrill of adventure tourism in the Northern Mariana Islands beckons the bold—those eager to dive into the depths of its azure waters, trek the emerald embrace of its forests, or conquer the towering presence of its volcanic landscapes. These experiences, rich with the promise of adrenaline and discovery, are the jewels in the CNMI's crown of natural wonders.

Nevertheless, with the surge of visitors seeking these thrills comes the need for a vigilant eye on safety and environmental care. The islands face the challenge of ensuring that every rope swing over a jungle ravine and every dive into the ocean's depths is a pulse-raising moment and a secure one. It is a task that demands rigorous safety checks, top-notch equipment, and guides who are not just adventure enthusiasts but also custodians of visitor well-being and environmental guardians.

Educating those who come to seek thrills is crucial. It is not just about equipping them with safety gear but about instilling a mindset that respects the delicate balance of the ecosystems they are about to enter. The guides, the local heroes of these escapades, must be adept at imparting wisdom about the islands' precious ecology alongside their safety briefings.

In the shadow of potential hazards, the CNMI's readiness to respond to emergencies is as critical as the thrill of adventure. This preparedness is not just about having a plan on paper; it is about drills, about knowing that if the unforeseen strikes, there is a well-oiled machine of a rescue operation ready to spring into action.

Insurance is not the most exciting topic in a conversation about adventure, but the safety net underpins the industry. Operators must be covered adequately and comprehensively to safeguard their businesses and the adventurers they serve.

Sustainability is the backbone of adventure tourism here. The islands' natural beauty is finite, and the thrill of today's adventure should not become the regret of tomorrow's loss. This means the footprints left behind should be as light as possible, preserving the CNMI's beauty for future thrill-seekers.

In the grand scheme, the CNMI's embrace of adventure tourism is not just about selling an experience but crafting a legacy of responsible, exhilarating exploration. It is about assuring that the islands remain a sanctuary where adventure is served with a generous side of safety and sustainability. This careful dance between offering excitement and ensuring preservation will keep the heart of adventure tourism beating strong in the Northern Mariana Islands.

Cruise Ship Tourism: A Surge of Visitors and the Ripple Effect

The arrival of a cruise ship in the Northern Mariana Islands is a spectacle of modern travel where a floating city docks and its inhabitants descend to explore the islands' charms. This form of tourism brings a surge of visitors, often overwhelming in numbers, who pour into local markets, beaches, and attractions, eager to consume the essence of the CNMI in a matter of hours before they depart for their next port of call.

This influx of cruise ship passengers can be likened to a sudden tide that washes over the islands, bringing economic tidings that are both beneficial and challenging. The economic injection is immediate—local vendors see a spike in sales, tour operators are fully booked, and the buzz in the air is palpable. However, this sudden wave of economic activity must be managed to prevent it from eroding the foundations of the islands' charm and sustainability.

Arriving simultaneously in sheer numbers, visitors test the limits of the CNMI's infrastructure. Streets become crowded, services are stretched thin, and the tranquility that defines the islands can momentarily dissipate. The challenge for the CNMI is to harness the positive aspects of this surge while mitigating the strain it places on local resources and the environment.

Local businesses, from souvenir shops to eateries, must prepare for the ebb and flow of cruise ship schedules, which can be as unpredictable as the ocean. On days when the ports are busy, the islands come alive with the energy of commerce. On others, the silence left in the wake of the ships can be unnervingly stark. The key for these businesses is to find balance and not become wholly dependent on the uncertain tides of cruise ship itineraries.

The environmental impact of cruise ships also cannot be ignored. The pristine waters and landscapes that draw visitors to the CNMI are at risk if not protected against potential pollution and the wear and tear of overuse. A unified endeavor by every involved party is essential to guarantee that the ecological impact of these ships and their guests is minimized to the greatest extent feasible.

In the broader context of managing tourism, the CNMI needs to reflect on the societal effects of cruise ship tourism. The islands' distinct culture and daily life are at risk of being overshadowed by tourists seeking a brief, pre-packaged experience of the islands' cultural offerings. Maintaining the genuineness of the local lifestyle is crucial, as is ensuring that interactions between visitors and residents are conducted with respect and contribute positively to both parties.

Cruise ship tourism presents a complex scenario that requires strategic planning and adaptive management. The goal is to welcome the positive economic impacts while maintaining the integrity of the islands' infrastructure, environment, and culture. It is about ensuring that the surge of visitors uplifts rather than overwhelms, leaving both the guests and the hosts looking forward to the next arrival with anticipation rather than apprehension.

Voluntourism: Helping or Hurting?

In the Northern Mariana Islands, the intersection of altruism and exploration has potential in voluntourism—a concept where visitors aim to leave a positive mark through volunteer work. While the intent behind such travel is commendable, the real-world outcomes in the CNMI can be a complex mix of benefits and burdens.

The influx of voluntourists to the CNMI introduces a wave of energy and workforce to various community projects. These volunteers, driven by good intentions, engage in a range of activities, such as cleaning beaches and teaching in schools, aiming to benefit the local community. In ideal situations, their efforts can bridge gaps and support areas lacking resources.

However, the concept of voluntourism is not without its drawbacks. It has prompted debate over the real and lasting impact of these volunteers. For example, there is the concern that their efforts may only offer short-term solutions that do not align with the community's long-term goals, leading to more disruption than help. Additionally, there is the worry that such programs might unintentionally overshadow local labor or create a reliance on outside assistance.

Additionally, the dynamics of voluntourism often raise questions about the actual motivation behind the volunteers' presence. Is the work genuinely supporting the local community, or is it more about the volunteers' experience and satisfaction? This is not just about semantics; it is about ensuring that the purported aid does not devolve into a self-centered pursuit, trivializing the locals' genuine challenges.

To harness the positives of voluntourism, the CNMI must strategically navigate this minefield. The success of these programs must be measured not by the number of volunteers or the hours logged but by the sustained positive change they foster in the community. This requires a commitment to community-driven projects, prioritizing the islands' long-term development goals, and operating with the utmost respect for local culture and society.

The CNMI is pivotal in determining the role of voluntourism within its community, aiming to weave it in without unraveling its social fabric. The success of this integration hinges on creating volunteer initiatives that are not just benevolent but also knowledgeable and effectively executed. The goal is to ensure voluntourism leaves a positive imprint of empowerment and respect rather than unintended damage or exploitation.

The tourism sector in the Northern Mariana Islands is complex and varied. Each form of tourism presents its advantages and issues. The effects range broadly from the economic boost and potential cultural watering down of mass tourism to the community strengthening and environmental focus of ecotourism. Cultural tourism in the CNMI strikes a delicate balance between preserving heritage and avoiding commercialization. Meanwhile, adventure tourism offers exhilarating experiences while emphasizing the need for safety and environmental conservation.

Cruise ship tourism injects substantial economic activity and stresses infrastructure and environmental resources, necessitating strategic planning and management. Voluntourism presents an opportunity for cultural exchange and community service but requires careful implementation to ensure that help is not hindered.

The vital need for a balanced approach is at the heart of tourism discussions in the CNMI. The islands are at a significant juncture, with the potential to shape the direction of their tourism industry. The choices made today will echo into the future, affecting the islands' social, cultural, and environmental heritage.

Government officials, industry stakeholders, and the wider community need to foster a tourism model that is sustainable, considerate, and beneficial for everyone involved. The enticing depictions offered to tourists need to be more reflective of the islanders' actual experiences, ensuring that the allure and culture promoted in travel literature do not come at the cost of the local community's well-being.

In considering the various forms of tourism and their societal effects, it becomes clear that the future direction is determined by visitors to the CNMI and its residents. Developing strategies and actions emphasizing enduring welfare over immediate benefits allows the Northern Mariana Islands to manage tourism as a tool used thoughtfully and responsibly. This approach aims to forge a future that is both flourishing and sustainable and that faithfully represents the essence of the islands.

Chapter 15

Opportunities for Change: Empowerment and Grassroots Initiatives

In the shadow of the revelations from Chapter 14, we approach a sobering truth—the current trajectory of tourism in the Northern Mariana Islands is untenable. Chapter 15, "Opportunities for Change: Empowerment and Grassroots Initiatives," unfolds as a stark admonition, an indictment of the status quo, and a call to action that cannot be ignored.

The scars of exploitation and neglect mar the landscape we have traversed thus far. Each tourism model, lauded for its economic promise, has also contributed to a creeping malaise that has eroded these islands' cultural fabric and natural splendor. The economic windfalls, once celebrated, now ring hollow against the growing chorus of dissent, highlighting the need for a drastic reevaluation.

Amidst this dire scenario, the need for transformative change is glaring. The strategies that have driven tourism development are now under scrutiny, their deficiencies casting long shadows over the islands' future. The callous commodification of culture, environmental degradation, and social dislocation wrought by unchecked tourism expansion are symptoms of a deeper malaise that demands urgent rectification.

Central to this discourse is the stark underrepresentation of local communities. Their marginalized voices, which carry the wisdom of genuine sustainability, must no longer be relegated to the periphery of tourism discourse. The disempowerment they suffer is a festering wound, one that undermines the potential for a tourism industry that is equitable and respectful.

Grassroots initiatives emerge as glimmers of optimism within this challenging environment, confronting the herculean struggle against deep-rooted interests and the sluggishness of a defective system. These movements represent the community's determination as they contend with the vast task of steering the colossal force of conventional tourism methods in a new direction.

As we navigate the unfolding realities, we are compelled to face harsh truths about the consequences of stagnancy. It is a journey that explores what could be achieved with the boldness to break away from outdated models. This chapter is not simply a testament to what may come; it is an impassioned call for transformative action for the Northern Mariana Islands to reclaim control of their future from a tourism paradigm that has exacted a hefty toll.

Education is commonly heralded as a vital instrument for empowerment and a fundamental element for sustainable development within the tourism industry. However, the situation in the Northern Mariana Islands starkly contrasts this ideal. Educational initiatives aimed at instilling sustainable practices among the local people frequently encounter the harsh wall of immediate economic necessities, resulting in a half-hearted or token implementation of these practices. The pressing need to make ends meet typically eclipses the perceived indulgence of long-term environmental considerations, casting doubts on such educational programs' real-world impact and viability.

Educational programs that empower residents frequently fail to address the entrenched economic dependencies that bind the community to unsustainable tourism practices. These programs can be met with skepticism, as locals may view them as idealistic notions that do not align with the harsh realities of their day-to-day struggles for economic survival.

The push to transform locals into entrepreneurs through workshops and training encounters challenges. Although well-meaning, these initiatives can underestimate residents' complexities, such as a lack of capital or support to launch their businesses. The tourism market is already saturated with foreign investment and established players, making it difficult for local start-ups to break through.

Moreover, educational tourism, intended as a bridge for cultural exchange, can inadvertently perpetuate a one-sided narrative. Instead of fostering genuine mutual learning, it can reduce the rich tapestry of the islands' heritage to a simplified and consumable product for tourists. This approach risks diluting the authenticity of the cultural experience, offering visitors only a superficial understanding and leaving locals as mere performers in their land.

While designed to elevate the community's influence in tourism, these initiatives often underscore the systemic issues. The local population remains on the periphery of an industry exploiting the islands' resources and culture, with only marginal input from those most impacted by these ventures.

Despite the charm of the Northern Mariana Islands, those engaged in grassroots efforts for a fair share in the tourism industry are met with significant challenges. Instances where grassroots movements have effectively influenced the tourism sector are rare and tend to be eclipsed by larger, commercially dominant entities that hold sway over the industry. The relative infrequency of these grassroots triumphs emphasizes the considerable imbalance in resources and clout, which often skews the playing field against community-based projects.

The involvement of non-governmental organizations (NGOs) in the tourism landscape is complex and contradictory. While they are often envisioned as champions for sustainable tourism, there is a risk that their efforts could foster reliance or promote ideals that clash with local traditions and values. The impact of NGOs, while potentially transformative, carries the risk of overshadowing indigenous cultures in the name of progress and conservation.

Community decision-making processes are another area of contention. The theoretical model of inclusive participation in guiding tourism development is often a far cry from reality. Local voices are routinely stifled by bureaucratic red tape and the political clout of multinational tourism operators. The decisions that ultimately shape the trajectory of tourism development tend to be made in boardrooms rather than in community halls, leaving the actual stakeholders—the island residents—on the periphery of the planning process that profoundly affects their homeland.

The persistent challenges faced by grassroots movements and community involvement in the Northern Mariana Islands reveal the underlying systemic barriers to equitable tourism development. These barriers highlight the need for a seismic shift in attitude and approach if true empowerment and sustainable change are to be achieved.

In the shadow of the Northern Mariana Islands' thriving tourism industry lies a stark reality—the Sustainable Development Goals (SDGs) often appear as little more than an idealistic framework, overshadowed by the immediate gains of unchecked tourism development. The lofty ambitions of the SDGs to foster responsible consumption, protect life below water, and ensure sustainable communities stand in stark contrast to the ground realities where profit margins often take precedence over sustainable practices.

The inclusion of the SDGs in tourism rhetoric is frequently met with skepticism by locals who witness the widening gap between the islands' economic interests and ecological needs. Promises of sustainable development and environmental stewardship often ring hollow when contrasted with the actual degradation of coral reefs, exploitation of natural resources, and the marginalization of local populations in favor of tourist-centric projects.

Moreover, the very essence of the SDGs, which calls for an end to poverty and a push for decent work and economic growth, seems at odds with the volatile nature of tourism jobs. These positions, often low-wage and lacking in security, contribute to economic disparities rather than alleviate them, challenging the notion that tourism is a golden ticket to achieving the SDGs on the islands.

Integrating the SDGs into the tourism sector requires a fundamental shift in priorities—where long-term sustainability is not sacrificed at the altar of short-term economic gain. For the Northern Mariana Islands, this would mean a stringent reassessment of how tourism can be realigned to truly support global goals without falling into the trap of performative actions and token gestures that fail to deliver tangible results.

The evolving landscape of the Northern Mariana Islands' tourism sector is not without its sparks of innovation, though they often seem like flickers in the dark, struggling to find oxygen in an atmosphere stifled by the status quo. Technological advancements have the potential to support sustainable tourism, yet their implementation is frequently obstructed by limited resources and resistance from established operators who favor traditional, less sustainable methods.

New business models for small-scale tourism enterprises offer a glimmer of hope for more personalized and responsible travel experiences. These models aim to decentralize the tourism industry, giving power back to local communities and entrepreneurs. However, these innovative approaches often face uphill battles for recognition and market share against the backdrop of mass tourism juggernauts that dominate the industry.

Leveraging crowdfunding and social media platforms offers a contemporary toolkit for advocates of grassroots initiatives, allowing them to circumvent typical financial obstacles by reaching out directly to a worldwide audience. Nevertheless, this approach is laden with its hurdles. It demands adept narrative crafting and digital proficiency to pierce through the clutter and secure the necessary engagement and backing in an often indifferent and saturated digital realm.

Each innovation holds the promise of beneficial transformation within the tourism sector of the Northern Mariana Islands. However, it is uncertain whether these emerging possibilities will kindle a lasting movement toward sustainability or be extinguished by the deep-rooted forces that have traditionally steered the course of tourism growth.

The Northern Mariana Islands, a landscape ripe with cultural wealth, stand on the precipice of opportunity where tourism could illuminate the path for cultural revival. However, the Chamorro and Carolinian cultures receive only passing nods within the broader tourism narrative, overshadowed by the more widely recognized Polynesian influences. The potential for these indigenous cultures to enrich the tourist experience with deep, meaningful interactions remains largely untapped, as visitors encounter the local customs and traditions primarily through sporadic festivals or specially curated events.

The platforms that should be bastions of cultural storytelling and heritage preservation are too often marginalized, reducing what could be a continuous stream of cultural exchange to mere trickles that appear fleetingly and too infrequently. As a result, the true essence of these cultures is diluted, their vibrant diversity subsumed by a more homogenous and marketable image.

Tourists often experience only a cursory glance at the islands' cultural richness, gaining a limited understanding of their true depth and meaning. This approach deprives visitors of a meaningful connection with the islands' cultural tapestry and limits the local communities from fully showcasing and preserving their heritage.

Preserving cultural authenticity in the wake of widespread tourism is a daunting task. The distinct Chamorro and Carolinian lifestyles, with their unique practices and beliefs, are at risk of being overshadowed by the tourism sector's inclination towards a more generic, globally familiar cultural narrative. The struggle involves more than just safeguarding history; it ensures the islands' cultural essence remains lively and integral to their tourism appeal.

In reimagining tourism to serve as a true proponent of cultural preservation, the Northern Mariana Islands can forge a path that intertwines preserving its unique cultural heritage with the visitor experience. This initiative goes beyond mere economic benefits—it is about instilling a sense of cultural pride and ensuring that the islands' heritage is showcased for entertainment and honored, taught, and celebrated as an intrinsic part of the islands' allure. This form of cultural tourism holds the potential to entertain, educate, and preserve the rich cultural legacies of the Chamorro and Carolinian peoples.

Environmental stewardship in tourism often clashes with the grim consequences of ecological damage. Eco-friendly initiatives, while present, do not always penetrate the deeper issues of resource exploitation and environmental harm. The effort to spread environmental awareness through tourism is commendable but tends to be overshadowed by practices that prioritize profit over planet health.

Policies aiming to minimize the ecological impact of tourism exist, but they struggle with implementation and enforcement. Sustainable infrastructure, such as waste management and renewable energy, is not as widespread as it needs to be, leading to a tourism industry that does not fully live up to its sustainable promises.

Tourism must undertake a more unified and deliberate approach to align authentically with environmental conservation principles. All parties must unite behind a vision of tourism that is sustainable in practice, not just in promise, safeguarding the natural world for the enjoyment of future generations.

The tourism sector finds itself at a critical point, necessitating urgent action to cultivate resilience against diverse challenges, including economic shifts and the pervasive threat of climate change. The Northern Mariana Islands must acknowledge the fragility of their reliance on traditional tourism models and urgently seek varied strategies to bolster economic stability.

The stark reality is that an over-reliance on a limited range of tourism-related income streams has left the local economy vulnerable to the unpredictable tides of global tourism dynamics and environmental catastrophes. There is a pressing need to diversify, identify, and invest in alternative tourism niches and experiences that can offer a more robust economic buffer.

Local community-driven methods for disaster management and climate adaptation are being recognized as essential. Past experiences have shown that centralized disaster management plans are often inadequate in addressing the specific needs of local communities. A paradigm shift toward empowering local communities, allowing them to lead and engage in planning and responsive measures, will likely yield more effective and enduring solutions.

Likewise, the infrastructure that supports tourism must be scrutinized and re-engineered with the future in mind. What was once deemed adequate now appears dangerously inadequate in the face of intensifying environmental events. A new vision for resilient tourism infrastructure should include not just reactive measures but proactive strategies — developing systems built to endure, adapt, and respond proactively to the emerging challenges of our time.

Confronting these daunting realities, the Northern Mariana Islands stand poised to embark on a transformative path. By re-evaluating long-standing practices and adopting innovative and forward-looking strategies, they can pave the way for a resilient, diverse, sustainable tourism industry equipped to prosper in the face of future uncertainties.

The potential for synergistic collaboration remains untapped mainly and under stress in the complex mosaic of the Northern Mariana Islands' tourism industry. The landscape reveals a glaring disconnection between the government's strategies, the private sector's profit motives, and the sustainability goals of local communities.

State entities often propose elaborate schemes for cooperation, but these plans tend to become entangled in red tape and conflicting interests, sidelining the communities they aim to support. Corporations, with their eyes on immediate financial gains, can neglect the enduring environmental and cultural impacts their operations engender. Meanwhile, the indigenous populations watch as their cultural legacy and natural heritage are reshaped by forces that seem indifferent to their fates.

Global partnerships, touted as vehicles for exchanging sustainable tourism practices, can become exercises in imposing standardized policies that ignore the islands' distinct character. These relationships should be mutualistic, yet there is a danger that they might devolve into exploitative arrangements, siphoning local resources and self-determination while offering little in return.

Tourists, central to the industry's vitality, are rarely engaged as genuine stakeholders in the islands' future. While they are drawn to the islands' unique cultural and natural allure, they are not often educated on the true extent of their impact or how they might contribute to the islands' enduring health. Instead of being empowered as agents of change, they remain as consumers of momentary pleasures, their potential for a positive legacy left untapped.

Amidst a backdrop where authentic cooperation could lead to a sustainable and fair tourism industry, current attempts at partnership are piecemeal, frequently only skin-deep, and sometimes wholly for show. The challenge is not in working together but in its practical realization. To unlock the full promise of their tourism sector, the Northern Mariana Islands need a shift in approach—one that genuinely values concerted, effective collaboration over the facade of agreement. Only with such a transformation can the islands aspire to cultivate a tourism paradigm that is inclusive, resilient, and genuinely sustainable.

As the Northern Mariana Islands contend with the diverse impacts of tourism, the significance of stringent monitoring and evaluation becomes increasingly apparent. The need for robust assessment tools and methodologies is acute in a climate where initiatives are often launched with fanfare but followed up with silence. Nevertheless, there is a persistent shortfall in applying such mechanisms, leading to an opaque understanding of what truly benefits the islands and their people.

Community feedback, which should be the cornerstone of any tourism-related project, often becomes an afterthought, sidelined in favor of top-down decision-making. The din of commerce and construction drowns out the voices of those most affected by tourism development. Without their insights, purported improvements can miss the mark, failing to address the core needs and desires of the islanders.

Transparency and accountability, the watchwords of ethical governance, seem to evaporate in the heat of the industry. Projects shrouded in secrecy move forward with neither the clarity of intention nor the scrutiny of a process they rightly demand. This cloak of ambiguity undermines the community's trust and casts a long shadow over the legitimacy of development endeavors.

The current state of monitoring and evaluation in the islands' tourism sector is a patchwork, with gaps where accountability should be. Data, when collected, is rarely dissected with a critical eye, and success is often measured by quantity over quality—how many tourists arrived, not the lasting impact of their stay.

In this environment, the call for a systematic overhaul of how tourism initiatives are assessed is not just a suggestion but a dire necessity. Without it, the islands risk perpetuating a cycle of unchecked growth and unheeded consequences, where the actual cost of tourism is tallied not in revenue but in lost cultural wealth and environmental degradation.

An investment in rigorous monitoring and evaluation systems is indispensable for a future where tourism serves the islands and not vice versa. Only then can the Northern Mariana Islands chart a course toward a tourism industry that's lucrative but also sustainable, equitable, and reflective of the community's vision.

As the final pages of this discussion turn, the future of tourism in the Northern Mariana Islands stands at a critical threshold. The vision for the coming years is not one painted with broad strokes of unfettered optimism. Instead, it is tinged with the sobering hues of reality—a future that acknowledges both the potential and the precariousness of the islands' tourism sector.

The challenges ahead are neither small nor simple. The Northern Mariana Islands grapple with the need to attract visitors while preserving the essence that makes them worth visiting. As the world's climate patterns shift and seas rise, the vulnerability of this island paradise becomes painfully clear. The infrastructure, strained by the current levels of tourism, may falter under the projected increase unless significant changes are made. The vibrant cultural fabric risks being frayed by the homogenizing forces of globalized tourism models.

Potential solutions do exist, though they require a steadfast commitment and a willingness to innovate. Sustainable practices must move from the periphery to the center of tourism strategies. Community-based tourism, which empowers residents and respects cultural integrity, needs to be more than a niche—it must become the norm. Moreover, education must play a pivotal role in shaping a tourism industry that values environmental stewardship as much as economic gain.

The role of the next generation is particularly critical. They inherit a legacy of the triumphs and the failures of current practices. It is upon their shoulders that the responsibility will fall to either continue down a path of shortsighted gains or to chart a new course that ensures the long-term viability of tourism. They must be equipped with the wisdom of their forebears and the tools to navigate and negotiate the complexities of a global industry.

Therefore, the future of tourism in the Northern Mariana Islands is a narrative still being written. It is a tale that could either extol the virtues of foresight and adaptability or be a cautionary chronicle of missed opportunities. The islands stand at a juncture that demands action, and the chosen direction will resonate through generations.

The importance of empowerment cannot be overstated. It is a linchpin in transforming tourism into a force that supports rather than subjugates. Empowerment is the bedrock upon which sustainable practices must be built, ensuring that the local populace is not merely a backdrop for tourists' experiences but an active participant in shaping their future.

Grassroots movements rise to the forefront in the struggle for sustainable tourism, symbolizing the perseverance and ingenuity of the community, even as they face the consequences of tourism's footprint. These efforts grapple with formidable obstacles, battling against the weight of established powers and systemic sluggishness. Nevertheless, their presence speaks to the relentless determination of those who understand that their homeland's well-being cannot be traded away.

The conversation reaches a decisive moment, beckoning all tourism sector stakeholders to step forward. A shared duty falls on everyone from government officials to business owners, craftspeople to global financiers, tourists to cultural custodians. Together, we must safeguard against pursuing profit at the expense of sustainable practices.

The future of tourism in the Northern Mariana Islands stands at a critical threshold, replete with hurdles yet ripe with opportunities for meaningful advancement. This crucial trek demands bravery, partnership, and a dedication to transformative change that respects historical roots while fearlessly pursuing new horizons. The outcome of this transformation is not yet written — it rests in the hands of today's inhabitants and the generations to follow. The imperative for resolute action is immediate; the direction tourism will take in the Northern Mariana Islands teeters on a knife-edge.

Chapter 16

Reimagining Local Participation: From Spectators to Beneficiaries

In the picturesque Northern Mariana Islands, where tourism flourishes as a primary economic driver, a crucial aspect often remains in the shadows: the role and participation of the local communities. Despite their significant contributions to the islands' cultural and natural allure, these communities are more observers than active participants in the tourism narrative. This reality underscores a vital need for a fundamental shift in perspective. Far from being mere scenic backdrops, the local inhabitants must be recognized and empowered as central stakeholders in the tourism industry.

The economic landscape of the tourism industry presents a stark contrast between its overall profitability and the limited financial benefits that trickle down to the local populace. Despite their integral role in sustaining the islands' heritage and environment, locals often find themselves excluded from the more lucrative aspects of the industry. This economic disparity manifests in limited access to sustainable employment opportunities, restricted entry into tourism-related entrepreneurship, and a heavy reliance on external entities that dominate the industry's infrastructure.

Alongside economic disparities, there is a notable cultural and social marginalization of the local communities. The rich cultural heritage of the Northern Mariana Islands, brimming with unique traditions and stories, is frequently underutilized or misrepresented in the tourism sector. Instead of being authentically integrated, local cultures are often reduced to mere attractions, lacking the depth and respect they deserve. This marginalization not only undermines the community's role but also robs tourists of experiencing the genuine cultural richness of the islands.

Compounding these challenges are the political and policy barriers that further entrench the marginalization of locals in the tourism industry. Policies and decisions in the sector often disproportionately favor multinational corporations and foreign investors, sidelining the needs and voices of the local populace. Legislative gaps, bureaucratic complexities, and a lack of adequate local representation in decision-making processes lead to a tourism model prioritizing external interests over local empowerment and cultural authenticity.

This landscape of the tourism industry in the Northern Mariana Islands, marked by economic, social, and political disparities, calls for an urgent reassessment and a concerted effort to reposition and empower local communities. The industry can only achieve a balance that benefits these vibrant islands' economy and cultural integrity through this fundamental shift.

The imperative for inclusive participation in the Northern Mariana Islands' tourism industry becomes increasingly evident when examining the components of economic resilience, cultural integrity, and community well-being. The involvement of local communities is not just a token gesture toward inclusivity; it is a cornerstone for building a sustainable tourism model.

Economic resilience in tourism is significantly enhanced when locals are active participants. By engaging in various aspects of the industry, from service roles to management and entrepreneurship, locals can help create a more robust and diversified economic base.

This diversification is essential, particularly in times of global uncertainty, where reliance on external markets and investments can be volatile. A tourism industry grounded in the local economy fosters resilience, ensuring that tourism's benefits continue circulating within the local community even in challenging times.

The preservation of cultural integrity is another critical aspect of inclusive tourism. The Northern Mariana Islands are rich in unique traditions and cultural narratives that should be the highlight of any authentic tourist experience. Local participation ensures that these cultural elements are represented accurately and respectfully. This enhances the tourist experience and ensures that local cultures are preserved and celebrated rather than commodified and diluted.

Tourism profoundly impacts community well-being, often in ways that are not immediately visible. Inclusive participation ensures that the social and environmental fabric of the local community is respected and maintained. It involves making conscious choices about how tourism is developed, such as prioritizing eco-friendly practices and ensuring that tourism does not disrupt local life but enriches it.

To empower local communities effectively, a multifaceted approach is necessary. Central to this is the implementation of educational initiatives. These initiatives should be specifically tailored to meet the unique requirements of the tourism industry, providing locals with the essential skills to capitalize on various opportunities. Such programs should offer a comprehensive skill set, encompassing everything from hospitality management to eco-tourism and digital marketing expertise. This wide-ranging educational scope is crucial to address today's varied and evolving demands in the tourism industry.

Promoting local entrepreneurship is another vital strategy. Facilitating access to capital and business support can empower residents to start their tourism-related businesses. This could involve creating microfinance programs, offering business mentorship, and providing platforms for local entrepreneurs to connect with larger markets. By nurturing local entrepreneurship, the tourism industry can stimulate a more equitable economic environment where profits are widely distributed.

Policy reforms are also essential in encouraging local participation. Advocating for changes in laws and regulations can create a more conducive environment for locals to engage in tourism. This might include tax incentives for local businesses, land-use policies favoring local entrepreneurs, and regulations ensuring fair employment practices in the tourism sector.

These strategies are not standalone solutions but interconnected elements of a broader approach aimed at transforming the tourism industry into a catalyst for sustainable development, cultural preservation, and community well-being in the Northern Mariana Islands.

In the realm of local engagement in tourism, Tortuguero in Costa Rica stands as an exemplary model. This village has embraced eco-tourism, aligning its economic development with a strong commitment to environmental conservation (2019). Initially reliant on traditional fishing, the community has shifted to offering guided nature tours, emphasizing educating tourists about their unique ecosystem, particularly the vital sea turtle nesting grounds. This transition to eco-tourism sustains the local economy and encourages deep community involvement in environmental stewardship. Tortuguero's approach illustrates how tourism can be economically viable and ecologically beneficial when intertwined with environmental care.

The small town of Alberobello in Italy echoes a similar success story, renowned for its unique trulli buildings (Alexander, 2019). Locals have ingeniously integrated their rich cultural heritage into the tourism experience. By transforming their historic trulli homes into boutique accommodations and hosting workshops where tourists can immerse themselves in traditional Italian crafts and cuisine, Alberobello has created an authentic and sustainable tourist experience. This innovative approach has revitalized the town's economy and played a pivotal role in preserving and celebrating its cultural identity. Alberobello serves as a testament to the power of leveraging cultural heritage in tourism, showcasing how it can lead to sustainable economic development while preserving the authenticity of local traditions.

Drawing inspiration from Tortuguero and Alberobello, the Northern Mariana Islands could significantly benefit from adopting a similar community-centric approach to tourism. The islands can cultivate an economically robust, culturally enriching, and environmentally sustainable tourism sector by pivoting towards models that ensure local communities are active participants.

The challenge lies in addressing the concerns of established tourism operators, who may view increased community involvement as a potential disruption to their business models. The key is to demonstrate that integrating local communities can enrich the tourism experience, diversify economic benefits, and bolster the industry's sustainability. Initiating pilot projects that embody the essence of community-based tourism can serve as powerful examples, showcasing the feasibility and benefits of such approaches.

In essence, the experiences of Tortuguero and Alberobello illuminate a path for the Northern Mariana Islands, pointing towards a future where tourism strengthens the economy and reinforces the local community's social, cultural, and environmental fabric. Embracing this inclusive approach could reshape the islands' tourism industry into a resilient, sustainable, and deep-rooted cultural identity model.

Community-Based Tourism (CBT) stands as a beacon of how tourism can be restructured to benefit local communities directly. CBT revolves around the principles of involving local communities in the planning, management, and development of tourism in their region. This approach ensures that the economic benefits of tourism are widely distributed among the community members and that the tourism activities are aligned with the community's values and traditions.

CBT offers a pathway to develop tourism for the Northern Mariana Islands that respects and preserves the islands' unique cultural and natural heritage. It encourages sustainable tourism practices that prioritize the well-being of local communities and their environment. By adopting the CBT model, the Northern Mariana Islands can diversify their tourism offer, highlighting their unique Chamorro and Carolinian cultures and stunning natural landscapes in a respectful and sustainable way.

Implementing Community-Based Tourism is not without its hurdles. There is a substantial need to invest in community education and skill development to manage tourism activities effectively. Local communities must have the right tools and knowledge to take charge of tourism projects. Beyond initial training, continuous support and mentorship are crucial to help these communities understand and adapt to the ever-evolving dynamics of the tourism industry. Moreover, striking a balance between reaping economic gains from tourism and preserving the cultural and natural essence of the community is a nuanced endeavor. It demands meticulous planning and thoughtful management to ensure that tourism development is beneficial and sustainable.

Leveraging technology is another crucial aspect of empowering local communities in tourism. Digital platforms offer unprecedented opportunities for promoting local businesses and culture to a global audience. These platforms can market local tourism offerings, from unique cultural experiences to eco-tours, showcasing the Northern Mariana Islands' distinct identity.

While technology offers immense potential in promoting tourism, ensuring it does not dilute the cultural authenticity of the experiences portrayed is crucial. The digital world tends to commodify cultural elements, which can lead to a loss of their genuine essence. To prevent this, the development and management of digital content and marketing strategies must be in the hands of the local communities. Local communities are the most authentic guardians of their own cultural and traditional heritage, and their active participation is essential in ensuring that digital representations align closely with the realities of their culture. The digital portrayal can maintain its integrity by involving those who live and breathe these traditions daily, mirroring the community's genuine experiences and rich heritage.

Using digital technology can be a game-changer for local businesses in the Northern Mariana Islands. It opens doors to global markets and helps create new and diverse revenue sources. Harnessing digital platforms elevates the visibility of the islands' unique tourism offerings and empowers the local community. It allows them to take charge of how their rich cultural heritage and stories are shared with the world, ensuring they are presented respectfully and authentically.

Adopting Community-Based Tourism and leveraging technology are essential steps toward creating a more inclusive and sustainable tourism model in the Northern Mariana Islands. These approaches promise a future where tourism contributes to the islands' economic development and upholds and celebrates the unique cultural heritage and natural beauty of this remarkable region.

Also, engaging the youth in tourism development is a pivotal aspect of ensuring the longevity and relevance of the industry in the Northern Mariana Islands. The younger generation brings fresh perspectives, innovative ideas, and a deep understanding of modern trends, all essential for the tourism sector to evolve and thrive. Strategies such as offering educational scholarships in tourism-related fields, creating internship opportunities with local tourism businesses, and providing platforms for youth to voice their ideas and solutions for tourism development are crucial to attracting and retaining young talent. Additionally, showcasing successful youth-led tourism projects can inspire and motivate more young people to consider careers in this sector.

In addition, redefining success metrics in tourism involves shifting the focus beyond traditional economic indicators like visitor numbers and revenue. It calls for a more holistic approach that considers the local community's well-being and cultural and natural heritage preservation. New benchmarks might include measures of local employment created by tourism, the extent of community engagement in tourism planning, the level of cultural knowledge transmission to visitors, and indicators of environmental sustainability in tourism practices. These metrics provide a more comprehensive picture of the impact and success of the tourism industry.

In conclusion, this chapter emphasized a critical need to reshape the approach to local involvement in the Northern Mariana Islands tourism sector. The chapter argues for a more equitable tourism model that not only shares its benefits more fairly among the local community but also plays an active role in preserving the islands' unique cultural and natural heritage. From government entities to tourism businesses and local community members, stakeholders are urged to embrace inclusive and sustainable practices. This commitment is vital to fostering a tourism industry that not only stimulates economic growth but also enhances the lives of residents and protects their rich cultural and environmental heritage for the enjoyment and education of future generations.

Chapter 17

Economic Diversification: Beyond The Tourism Industry

In the shadow of idyllic beaches and tourist-laden streets, the Commonwealth of the Northern Mariana Islands (CNMI) faces an uncomfortable truth: its economy, precariously perched upon the unstable pillar of tourism, is vulnerable. Chapter 17 delves into this pressing issue, laying bare the economic challenges and uncertainties that loom over the CNMI's future. This chapter is not a celebration of success but a candid acknowledgment of over-reliance and its risks.

The islands' enchanting allure, drawing visitors from around the globe, has long been the cornerstone of their economic structure. However, this dependency has come at a cost. The widespread interruptions in global travel due to the COVID-19 pandemic have sharply exposed the risks associated with excessive dependence on a single economic sector. In the wake of such crises, the fragility of a tourism-dependent economy is not just a theoretical concern but a harsh reality that has left deep scars on the CNMI's economic landscape.

The journey towards economic diversification is not a straightforward one. It demands a critical evaluation of the CNMI's current economic model, a willingness to confront uncomfortable truths, and an unwavering commitment to charting a new course. Navigating this path requires more than just recognizing the need for change; it demands a resolute dedication to reshaping the economic future of the CNMI. The stakes are high: the economic resilience of the islands and the prosperity of their inhabitants rest on the successful exploration and cultivation of these new sectors. This venture is not merely a choice but a crucial step toward securing a sustainable and diverse economic landscape for the CNMI.

Diversification, therefore, is not a mere strategic choice but an economic lifeline. By expanding into different sectors, the CNMI can cushion itself against the ebb and flow of global tourism trends and other external shocks. A multifaceted economy offers a buffer, spreading risk and reducing the fallout from any sector's downturn. Beyond mere survival, diversification holds the promise of long-term benefits. It paves the way for sustainable growth, opening doors to new markets, fostering innovation, and creating a range of job opportunities that can elevate the overall standard of living for the CNMI's residents.

Moreover, a diversified economy can empower the local community, allowing for more equitable economic participation. It can break the cycle of dependency on external factors and build a more self-reliant economic framework. This shift can also align with and support the cultural and environmental values of the CNMI, ensuring that economic growth does not come at the expense of the islands' unique heritage and natural beauty.

For a sustainable economic future, CNMI must explore opportunities beyond tourism. This diversification will fortify the economy against global disruptions and broaden the base of opportunities for the local population. Several sectors show potential for development, such as agriculture, fishing, renewable energy, and digital services.

Agriculture: A Foundation for Diversification

In the CNMI, the hidden gem of agriculture waits to be fully realized. This sector, overshadowed by the dominant tourism industry, holds immense potential due to the islands' rich volcanic soil and favorable subtropical climate. However, the journey to harness this potential is riddled with challenges.

In the CNMI, the agricultural sector confronts a notable challenge due to the scarcity of arable land, a constraint inherent in the islands' geographical makeup. This difficulty is further intensified by the ever-present risk of natural calamities, especially typhoons, which severely threaten conventional farming. However, these hurdles do not mark the end of the road; instead, they create opportunities to adopt cutting-edge and innovative farming techniques.

Enter hydroponics and vertical farming – two key solutions to overcoming these hurdles. Hydroponics, a technique where plants are grown in a nutrient-rich water solution instead of soil, elegantly sidesteps the issue of scarce land (U.S. Department of Agriculture). This method efficiently uses limited space, enhances crop yields, and conserves water. Vertical farming, meanwhile, revolutionizes the concept of farming itself.

Arranging crops in vertically stacked layers in a controlled environment maximizes available space and shields plants from the harshness of unpredictable weather. This approach to agriculture turns the challenge of limited space into an advantage, harnessing technology and innovation to ensure productivity and resilience against the elements.

Adopting these advanced farming methods goes beyond merely addressing the CNMI's specific agricultural challenges. They embody a progressive attitude towards agriculture, harnessing technology to establish sustainable and productive farming systems amidst geographical and environmental limitations.

Exploring the cultivation of medicinal plants presents a noteworthy opportunity for the CNMI. In an era where demand for natural health products is surging, the islands could become an essential source of medicinal crops like turmeric, ginger, and aloe vera. Such a strategic shift would broaden the scope of the islands' agricultural sector and place them in a favorable position within the growing market for natural wellness products.

However, as the CNMI ventures into expanding its agricultural capabilities, it is imperative to tread this path with a deep commitment to sustainability. This approach involves farming methods that conserve resources, safeguard the local ecosystem, and maintain the islands' inherent natural allure. Embracing responsible agricultural practices and a pledge to nurture and preserve the CNMI's environmental heritage for generations is necessary. This holistic approach ensures that the islands' agricultural growth aligns with the ethos of environmental stewardship and sustainability.

In essence, agriculture represents more than just an alternative economic path for the CNMI. It is a chance to blend innovation with tradition, turn challenges into opportunities, and create a sustainable and resilient future that balances economic growth with environmental stewardship.

Sustainable Fishing and Mariculture: Balancing Economy with Ecology

The Northern Mariana Islands, graced with abundant marine biodiversity, face the challenge of balancing economic growth with ecological conservation, particularly in fishing and mariculture. The CNMI's commitment to sustainable fishing practices is not just an economic imperative but a pivotal factor in maintaining the delicate balance of its marine ecosystem. The region's diverse marine life, including groupers and snappers, offers both an economic opportunity and a conservation challenge. The journey to sustainable fishing is fraught with the perils of overfishing and habitat degradation, necessitating vigilant regulation and responsible practices.

Mariculture, also known as marine aquaculture, emerges as a crucial element in this equilibrium, offering sustainable solutions and new opportunities. This practice involves farming marine organisms such as fish, crustaceans, and seaweed in their natural environments, including open oceans, enclosed sections of the ocean, tanks, ponds, or raceways filled with seawater (Laird, 2003). The CNMI's potential for mariculture is considerable, offering an innovative approach to supplement natural fish stocks and meet local and global seafood demands. Cultivating species like groupers, snappers, lobsters, and various seaweeds expands the range of available marine products. When implemented with best practices and modern technology, mariculture in the CNMI can evolve into an environmentally sustainable and economically profitable venture, offering a new avenue for diversifying the islands' economy.

The economic benefits of a thriving marine industry in the CNMI are straightforward, providing a stable and diversified source of income. However, the ecological implications are equally crucial. Sustainable fishing and responsible mariculture practices contribute to the health of CNMI's local economy and the global marine ecosystem. This is increasingly important in a world facing climate change and biodiversity loss.

Successfully developing sustainable fishing and mariculture in the CNMI involves navigating a complex interplay between economic ambitions and ecological responsibility. The key to thriving in this sector lies in meticulous management, ongoing vigilance, and a profound appreciation of the ocean's importance in the worldwide ecosystem. The longevity and prosperity of the CNMI's marine sector will depend on its capacity to judiciously exploit marine resources while safeguarding their sustainability for future generations.

Renewable Energy Revolution: Leveraging Solar and Wind Power for Sustainable Economic Expansion

At a crucial juncture in its development, the CNMI faces the compelling imperative of embracing renewable energy, not merely as an eco-friendly initiative but as a cornerstone of economic independence. The islands' untapped solar and wind energy potential is evident, offering a clear path forward amidst the heavy reliance on costly imported fuel.

The CNMI's geographical blessings, with its abundant year-round sunshine, present a golden opportunity for solar power generation. However, this potential remains underutilized mainly, overshadowed by the islands' current dependence on expensive, imported diesel for power. Similarly, the consistent winds characteristic of the CNMI's oceanic climate offer fertile ground for wind energy development, a resource yet to be fully harnessed amidst traditional energy practices.

The transition from a fossil-fuel-dominated energy landscape to one rich in renewable resources requires a bold shift in perspective and policy. The examples of Kauai and Samso stand as beacons, showing the transformative power of renewable energy. Kauai has significantly reduced its reliance on external fuel sources through its expansive solar farm (Spector, 2023), while Samso has become an exemplary figure in wind energy utilization (Wear, 2020). However, these success stories highlight the substantial investment and policy changes CNMI needs to follow suit.

This pivot towards renewable energy is environmentally prudent and has substantial economic implications. By reducing energy costs and aligning with global carbon reduction efforts, CNMI can position itself as a leader in sustainable practices in the Pacific. Nevertheless, the journey to this renewable future is not without challenges, requiring comprehensive infrastructure, policy, and public mindset changes. The embrace of solar and wind energy is an essential step, not just a choice, for the economic and ecological well-being of CNMI.

Digital Services and Technological Growth: Harnessing Innovation for Economic Diversification

The shift towards a digital and technologically advanced economy offers a promising path for the CNMI, albeit fraught with complexities and critical considerations. The cornerstone of this transformation lies in establishing a solid digital infrastructure, a significant undertaking that demands substantial investment and strategic foresight. Such infrastructure is vital for drawing in remote businesses, digital nomads, and innovative tech firms, potentially revitalizing the CNMI's economy.

However, the challenges extend beyond mere infrastructure. A pressing need exists to cultivate digital literacy within the local populace, addressing the current shortfall in essential tech skills like coding, digital marketing, and data analytics. This endeavor is about attracting external investment and empowering locals to actively engage in the emerging digital economy. Initiatives such as local tech education programs, online learning partnerships, and perhaps even establishing a dedicated digital education institution are critical, yet they call for robust support and enduring commitment.

The CNMI can look to Malta as a case study. Malta's transformation into a tech hub, driven by attractive tax incentives and a supportive business environment, showcases a potential roadmap for the CNMI (Munford, 2016). However, this approach must be cautiously navigated, weighing the economic benefits against possible risks, including the potential commercialization of the islands at the expense of local culture and interests.

Moreover, integrating technology into the CNMI's economy must balance preserving its unique cultural heritage and environmental beauty. The risk here is that technological advancement could overshadow or even diminish the islands' cultural and natural treasures if not managed carefully. It is crucial that technological growth not only fosters economic diversification but also acts as a conduit for enhancing and safeguarding the CNMI's rich cultural and environmental heritage.

While embracing digital and technological advancements opens up new avenues for economic diversification in the CNMI, it requires careful and considerate implementation. This transition is about economic resilience and sustainability and preserving the cultural and environmental essence that makes the CNMI unique. The journey is challenging and complex, but it is a necessary step towards a more balanced and sustainable economic future for the islands.

The journey through the various sectors that promise economic diversification in the CNMI - agriculture, sustainable fishing, renewable energy, and digital services - has illuminated potential pathways for a more resilient economy. However, as we delve deeper into the complexities of economic diversification, we confront various challenges and necessary considerations that are integral to ensuring the success of this pivotal transition.

Investing in infrastructure forms the bedrock of efforts to diversify the economy. Developing robust physical and digital networks is crucial for the growth of new industries. However, in the CNMI, this investment is a financial allocation and strategic planning matter. The islands' unique environmental concerns and geographical limitations necessitate a careful approach to infrastructure development to ensure that it supports new industries without harming the delicate ecological balance.

Balancing modernization with environmental and cultural integrity is another significant challenge. Introducing new industries must be managed sensitively to preserve the CNMI's natural beauty and cultural heritage. This balance is challenging, as it often requires rethinking long-established practices and values in the face of modern economic demands.

Overcoming resistance to change in traditional sectors is a critical step towards diversification. Habitual ways of operating, skepticism towards new methods, and reluctance to depart from familiar practices can slow down the progress toward a diversified economy. This resistance is particularly pronounced in communities where traditional lifestyles have been predominant for generations.

Involving and empowering local communities is vital to successfully transitioning toward a diversified economy. This process means actively including community members in decision-making, fully grasping their unique needs and worries, and crafting development strategies that provide mutual benefits. Educating communities, enhancing their skills, and incorporating them into the planning process can build a bridge between innovative economic ventures and long-standing local customs. This approach fosters a collaborative atmosphere and instills a deep sense of ownership and partnership among the residents.

Navigating this intricate transition requires a carefully crafted policy framework. Government policies should incentivize the development of new sectors while protecting environmental and cultural assets. This could involve tax incentives for sustainable practices, funding for research in emerging industries, and streamlined processes to encourage investment.

Forming public-private partnerships is pivotal in this transformative process. Engaging with private sector partners can introduce vital expertise and capital, thus fast-tracking the growth of emerging industries. These collaborations must be structured through transparent and reciprocal agreements, safeguarding the interests of the CNMI and its citizens.

Engaging in international collaborations opens up opportunities for the CNMI to access new markets, technologies, and funding. It also allows sharing experiences and learning from the successes and challenges of other regions undergoing similar transitions.

Regular monitoring and evaluation of diversification strategies are critical. They ensure that these strategies are achieving their intended economic, social, and environmental goals and allow for adjustments where necessary. This ongoing evaluation process is crucial for accountability and provides valuable insights for future policy-making.

The path to economic diversification in the CNMI is fraught with challenges; it is a necessary journey. The vulnerabilities of a tourism-dependent economy, highlighted by recent global crises, underscore the urgency of this transition. The CNMI stands at a crossroads where strategic decisions and careful planning can pave the way for a more resilient and sustainable economic future.

The journey toward economic diversification in the CNMI, marked by its complex challenges and opportunities, can draw valuable insights from global case studies. Islands worldwide have charted unique paths in diversifying their economies, offering a blend of inspiration and cautionary tales for the CNMI. These examples of successful diversification demonstrate the various strategies and approaches that have enabled island economies to thrive beyond their traditional sectors.

Iceland: Once heavily dependent on fishing, Iceland transformed its economy by developing geothermal and hydropower resources (Aldred, 2008). This shift created a sustainable energy sector and spurred growth in technology and tourism, making Iceland a prime example of successfully leveraging natural resources.

Singapore: As a trading port, Singapore diversified into manufacturing, finance, and technology (Chin, 2023). Its strategic location and investment in education and infrastructure have made it a global economic hub, illustrating the power of strategic planning and innovation in an island economy.

Malta: Known for its tourism, Malta has recently expanded into digital services and gaming, attracting tech companies through favorable policies (Cassar, 2023). This move showcases the potential of small island economies to tap into the digital and service sectors.

The experiences of these islands offer a wealth of knowledge for the CNMI as it embarks on its diversification journey. There is a lesson from Iceland in harnessing natural resources and innovatively transforming them into sustainable and profitable sectors. Singapore's story teaches the importance of strategic location utilization, coupled with heavy investment in human capital and infrastructure. This approach can transform a simple geographical advantage into a multifaceted economic powerhouse. Meanwhile, Malta's pivot towards digital services and gaming sectors highlights the potential to adapt to global market trends and create a niche in the burgeoning tech industry.

For the CNMI, these case studies underscore the necessity of a tailored approach to economic diversification. They must capitalize on their unique natural beauty, strategic location, and cultural heritage while embracing modernization and technological advancements. Learning from these global examples, the CNMI can craft strategies that foster economic growth and preserve and enhance its natural and cultural assets. Ensuring a balanced approach is vital in ensuring that economic diversification not only leads to financial stability but also enhances the quality of life for residents and preserves the environmental and cultural heritage for future generations.

In sum, Chapter 17 underscores the importance of the CNMI expanding beyond its heavy dependence on tourism, emphasizing the urgent need for economic diversification. This exploration reveals the potential within sectors such as agriculture, sustainable fishing, renewable energy, and digital services while acknowledging the complexities and challenges inherent in this transition.

The experiences of global counterparts like Iceland, Singapore, and Malta provide valuable insights into leveraging unique resources and adapting to changing economic landscapes. These case studies emphasize the importance of strategic planning, innovation, and community involvement.

For the CNMI, this path towards diversification is not just about economic resilience but about creating a sustainable and inclusive future that respects the islands' unique cultural and natural heritage. As the CNMI navigates this transformative journey, its choices will shape its economic future, offering opportunities for growth, sustainability, and a more balanced and prosperous society.

Chapter 18

Destination Rebranding and Marketing: Crafting the CNMI Image

In the ever-evolving world of global tourism, the branding of a destination is increasingly vital. This branding serves as an influential yet invisible force, shaping how potential tourists view a place, influencing their travel decisions, and being crucial for the economic success of a region's tourism sector; initiating a rebranding effort for the Northern Mariana Islands after COVID-19 is essential. The pandemic has altered the global travel landscape, affecting tourist preferences and revealing new challenges and opportunities.

As the CNMI emerges from these unique challenges, it is at a crucial juncture. The goal is to recover what was lost and redefine and transform the CNMI's presence in the world tourism market. This chapter examines the complex task of rebranding and marketing a destination, a process key to renewing the CNMI's allure in a world where travel habits and expectations have shifted dramatically. It will investigate how the CNMI can go beyond its conventional image by integrating its distinct cultural, natural, and historical attributes into a new, engaging narrative. This narrative must connect with the evolving global traveler demographic and the CNMI's fundamental values and identity. In an intensely competitive global tourism landscape, the CNMI's rebranding represents a marketing challenge and a strategic necessity vital for its future success and recognition in the international tourism sector.

Historically, the CNMI has been marketed primarily as a sun, sand, and sea destination – a tropical getaway characterized by its pristine beaches and clear waters. This image, while attractive, has become somewhat commonplace in a world brimming with similar offerings. Moreover, such a narrow focus fails to capture the full breadth of the islands' experiences and cultural richness. It is a narrative that has served well in the past, but in light of changing global trends, it risks rendering the CNMI indistinguishable from numerous other destinations.

This approach to branding has overlooked a critical aspect of the CNMI's allure: its unique cultural identity. Despite its potential to offer a rich, immersive experience through its diverse indigenous cultures and historical influences, these elements have been underrepresented in its tourism narrative. The CNMI's cultural heritage, shaped by Spanish, German, Japanese, and American influences, alongside the indigenous Chamorro and Carolinian traditions, presents a multifaceted story that is yet to be fully leveraged in its tourism marketing.

While successfully attracting tourists, the emphasis on traditional beach tourism has inadvertently limited the CNMI's appeal. This one-dimensional portrayal does not do justice to the depth and diversity of the islands' cultural offerings, which could attract a broader audience seeking authentic cultural experiences. The rich traditions, historical sites, and cultural practices of the local communities are assets that could significantly enhance the islands' tourism appeal.

Moreover, this lack of cultural emphasis in the CNMI's tourism branding has implications beyond attracting visitors. It impacts the preservation and celebration of the islands' heritage. Integrating culture into the tourism strategy is not merely a marketing move but a commitment to showcasing the CNMI's authentic identity, fostering local pride, and protecting cultural heritage.

In rethinking the CNMI's brand image, there is a clear opportunity to shift from a purely beach-focused narrative to one encompassing the islands' cultural richness and history. This would set the CNMI apart in the competitive tourism market and contribute to a more sustainable and culturally respectful form of tourism.

Acknowledging the shift in concerns from health risks to a deeper appreciation for unique travel experiences, the CNMI's rebranding strategy post-pandemic holds even greater significance. With travelers now less focused on health risks and more on enriching travel experiences, the CNMI has a unique opportunity to redefine its appeal in the global tourism market.

This period presents an ideal time for the CNMI to diversify its image beyond the typical tropical paradise narrative. While its beautiful beaches and clear waters are significant assets, travelers' interest in immersive experiences that delve into local culture, history, and nature is growing. This changing preference calls for the CNMI to highlight its rich cultural heritage, diverse ecosystems, and unique traditions.

A successful rebranding effort should thus pivot towards showcasing the CNMI as a destination that offers more than just scenic beauty. It should highlight experiences that allow visitors to connect deeply with the local community, understand the islands' rich history, and engage in sustainable tourism practices. This approach would differentiate the CNMI from similar destinations and attract tourists looking for more meaningful and responsible travel options.

Additionally, rebranding can help tap into new market segments, such as eco-tourists, cultural enthusiasts, and adventure seekers. By promoting the CNMI's lesser-known attractions and stories, the tourism sector can appeal to a broader audience, enhancing its resilience and sustainability in a rapidly changing world.

The rebranding of the CNMI transcends mere recovery from the pandemic's aftermath. It represents an opportune moment for transformation and elevation in global tourism. Such a strategic pivot could culminate in a more dynamic, varied, and sustainable tourism industry, aligning with the changing preferences of today's travelers.

In redefining its brand, the CNMI must identify and leverage its unique selling propositions (USPs) – those features that set it apart from other destinations. A key element in this endeavor is integrating local culture and values into the brand image, making it distinct and deeply rooted in the essence of the islands.

Firstly, the CNMI's cultural heritage is a treasure trove of stories, traditions, and arts that can provide a rich backdrop for its tourism narrative. The islands offer a unique cultural tapestry from the ancient Chamorro and Carolinian cultures to the influences of Spanish, German, and Japanese historical periods. Promoting cultural festivals, indigenous crafts, traditional cuisines, and historical sites will enrich the tourist experience and foster a sense of pride and participation among local communities.

Nature and biodiversity are other significant USPs for the CNMI. The islands' lush landscapes, diverse marine life, and protected areas like the Marianas Trench Marine National Monument offer unparalleled opportunities for eco-tourism. Highlighting these natural wonders in a way that encourages preservation and sustainability can attract tourists who are increasingly conscious of their environmental impact.

The rebranding should consider contemporary elements, such as the CNMI's sustainability and community engagement efforts. Showcasing initiatives in renewable energy, conservation efforts, and community-led tourism projects can position the CNMI as a forward-thinking, responsible destination.

Through a strategic blend of cultural depth, natural beauty, and modern values, the CNMI can craft a compelling, multifaceted brand image. This image should captivate potential tourists and resonate with the local community, ensuring the branding is authentic and sustainable. The CNMI can redefine its place in the global tourism market by offering a rich, diverse, and meaningful experience beyond the conventional sun, sand, and sea narrative.

The rebranding journey for the CNMI begins with in-depth research and market analysis, delving into its target audience's evolving preferences and expectations. This crucial stage involves gathering data on various aspects such as tourist demographics, travel patterns, competitor landscapes, and emerging global tourism trends. Gathering insights from past visitors through surveys and focus groups is essential to comprehend what aspects tourists find appealing and valuable in a travel destination. This understanding will help identify the competitive strengths of the CNMI and areas where it can uniquely position itself.

Following the research, the focus shifts to conceptualizing a new brand identity. This step defines the key themes and messages at the heart of the CNMI's rebranding efforts. The chosen themes should resonate with the target audience and genuinely reflect the unique attributes of the CNMI – its cultural richness, natural beauty, and commitment to sustainable tourism. The creation of these themes involves crafting a narrative that tells a story about the destination and the enriching experiences it offers. This narrative should be engaging and authentic, encapsulating what the CNMI stands for.

The visual elements, including logos, color schemes, and imagery, need careful design to ensure they are appealing and memorable and convey the essence of CNMI's new brand identity. These elements should be versatile enough to be effective across various marketing platforms.

The process also involves stakeholders from across the tourism sector – including local communities, business owners, and government entities – to ensure the rebranding is inclusive and representative of diverse perspectives within the CNMI.

Once the new brand identity is in place, the implementation phase begins, accompanied by developing of a comprehensive communication strategy. This strategy details how the new brand will be introduced and promoted, utilizing a mix of marketing channels to effectively reach and engage the target audience.

An essential aspect of the rebranding effort is storytelling. Sharing real stories from the islands, its people, and visitors helps form an emotional connection with potential tourists, portraying the CNMI as more than just a vacation spot but a destination offering a rich, immersive experience.

The rebranding of the CNMI is a complex and layered process. It starts with pinpointing and comprehending the target demographic, crafting an engaging brand identity, and implementing a strategic communication plan. By emphasizing its distinct characteristics and involving the local community, the CNMI has the potential to reinvent its global tourism stance, attracting a broader and more varied group of visitors.

As the CNMI embarks on a new chapter in its tourism narrative, the marketing strategies for the revamped brand must be dynamic and multifaceted, combining the reach and relevance of digital platforms with the familiarity and impact of traditional methods.

Digital marketing approaches will play a pivotal role in this strategy. With their vast and varied user base, social media channels offer an excellent platform for engaging with potential visitors. Regular and consistent posts showcasing the natural beauty, cultural richness, and unique experiences of the CNMI can create an engaging and compelling online presence. Additionally, partnerships with influencers and travel bloggers can amplify this reach. Influencers, with their dedicated followers and credibility, can effectively communicate the essence of CNMI's brand, providing authentic endorsements.

Online campaigns, including targeted advertisements and email marketing, will be instrumental in reaching specific audiences. These campaigns can be tailored based on user interests, travel habits, and demographics, ensuring the messaging resonates with each segment. SEO strategies and engaging website content will enhance online visibility, drawing more visitors to CNMI's official tourism platforms.

While digital marketing offers vast potential, traditional marketing methods still hold significant value. Print media, including brochures, magazines, and flyers, can be effective, especially in travel agencies and expos. These materials provide tangible reminders of the destination and can be particularly appealing to specific demographic groups.

Television advertising remains a powerful tool as well. A well-produced TV commercial, capturing the allure of the CNMI, can reach a broad audience, creating a lasting impression. This approach is particularly beneficial for creating a sense of place and emotion, something that is sometimes less tangible in digital formats.

Participation in travel expos and trade shows is another crucial aspect. These events allow networking with industry professionals, building relationships with travel agents, and directly engaging with potential tourists. They are platforms for the CNMI to showcase its new brand identity and offerings, gaining direct feedback and insights from the travel community.

The CNMI must ensure a uniform brand message across various channels and platforms to implement these marketing strategies. Integrating digital and traditional marketing methods will ensure a comprehensive reach, catering to a diverse audience and maximizing the impact of the rebranding effort.

This blend of innovative digital strategies and time-tested traditional methods will position the CNMI effectively in the competitive tourism market, attracting new visitors while retaining its charm and unique appeal.

The endeavor to reshape the CNMI's tourism identity, deeply involving local communities, presents a complex yet promising landscape. The rebranding process must transcend beyond superficial engagement, involving local populations as active architects in reshaping the tourism narrative. This approach is essential to forge an authentic and enduring brand image that aligns with local ethos and visitor expectations.

Integrating local communities into this rebranding journey is more than a ceremonial inclusion; it demands a profound engagement that genuinely respects and reflects the nuances of local viewpoints. This depth of involvement is critical in developing a brand that mirrors the CNMI's unique essence and values. Neglecting local voices in this process risks cultivating a tourism brand that feels contrived and disconnected, failing to resonate with visitors and residents alike.

Navigating the promotion of the CNMI's cultural heritage while respecting local sensibilities is a crucial challenge. The aim is to showcase the culture without exploiting it, a task that requires careful navigation and ongoing dialogue with community stakeholders to ensure respectful and authentic representation.

Continual engagement with local communities is not a one-off task but an evolving conversation, ensuring that the branding remains adaptable and responsive to changing local sentiments and global trends. This strategy can help avoid issues in other destinations where tourism development leads to cultural misrepresentation or over-tourism.

Examining successful examples of community-involved tourism branding, such as in Bhutan and New Zealand, reveals the benefits of respectfully and genuinely integrating local culture into tourism. These examples demonstrate how a tourism brand can be distinctive and culturally sensitive, offering visitors an immersive experience while preserving local traditions.

For the CNMI, developing community-based tourism initiatives can be a crucial strategy. These initiatives can offer more equitable economic benefits from tourism and provide tourists with authentic, meaningful experiences. Potential initiatives include local-led tours, cultural experiences, and homestay programs, allowing visitors to engage directly with the CNMI's culture and people.

The goal of the CNMI is to create a synergy between tourism development and community well-being. By bringing local communities to the forefront of rebranding, the CNMI can craft an attractive tourism brand that reflects its people's values and aspirations. This strategy aims to redefine the islands' image while fostering a sustainable and harmonious future for its tourism sector.

Rebranding CNMI's tourism with a focus on sustainable and responsible practices requires a delicate balance between showcasing the region's allure and preserving its ecological and cultural essence.

At the core of this strategy is ecological and cultural sensitivity. With a growing global inclination towards sustainable travel, CNMI has the potential to emerge as a frontrunner in eco-tourism. This means more than just flaunting natural beauty; it is about adopting protective measures for these natural treasures. The goal is to draw tourists and engage them in meaningful conservation activities.

Eco-tourism should transcend being a mere promotional tool and embody a pledge to responsible travel that honors the environment and aids in its preservation. This could include options like environmentally friendly accommodations, initiatives for wildlife conservation, and educational tours that spread environmental consciousness. By weaving these aspects into CNMI's branding, the destination can attract eco-aware travelers and set benchmarks for sustainable tourism.

Preserving cultural heritage is equally critical. The CNMI's cultural richness differentiates it, but preserving this heritage is more than mere exhibition. It involves actively maintaining cultural practices, languages, and traditions. This could be achieved through showcasing cultural events, supporting local artisans, and offering genuine and respectful cultural experiences.

A significant hurdle in this path is avoiding over-commercializing eco-tourism and cultural experiences. The aim should be to establish a tourism model that nurtures rather than exploits CNMI's natural and cultural assets. This requires thoughtful planning and collaboration with environmental specialists, cultural custodians, and local communities.

The CNMI could look towards destinations that have successfully melded sustainable practices with their tourism models. Examples include places with limits on visitor numbers to protect delicate ecosystems or those with community-centric tourism where locals guide the portrayal and sharing of their culture.

By emphasizing eco-tourism and cultural preservation, CNMI can reshape its image as a destination offering an extraordinary travel experience and promoting responsible and sustainable tourism. Such a strategy will elevate CNMI's position in the global tourism market and safeguard its natural and cultural riches for future generations.

To effectively assess the rebranding success of the CNMI, a meticulous process of evaluation and modification is crucial. The use of specific metrics and methods is fundamental in determining the effectiveness of these efforts, providing data for informed decision-making and strategy adjustments.

Evaluating the influence of the CNMI's rebranding requires a comprehensive approach. This begins with measurable indicators, including a rise in tourist numbers, enhanced revenues in the tourism industry, and a larger market share. Such statistics give a concrete indication of the market reach and acceptance of the new brand. Nevertheless, these numerical data points alone are insufficient to understand the impact of rebranding fully.

Feedback mechanisms play a critical role. Both on-site and post-visit tourist surveys can provide invaluable insights into visitor perceptions and experiences. These surveys should explore overall satisfaction and how well the rebranded image aligns with the tourists' actual experiences. It is crucial to understand if the new branding resonates with the target audience and fulfills its promises.

Social media analytics offer another layer of insight. By monitoring hashtags, mentions, and engagement on platforms like Instagram, Twitter, and Facebook, CNMI can gauge public sentiment and the viral reach of its branding efforts. Social media acts as a real-time focus group, revealing what aspects of the rebranding are hitting the mark and which are not.

Review platforms like Trip Advisor and Google Reviews also serve as valuable feedback sources. These platforms can indicate how well the new brand image translates into actual tourist experiences. High ratings and positive reviews can signal successful rebranding, while negative feedback can pinpoint improvement areas.

In addition to these direct measures, indirect indicators such as increased investment in the tourism sector, enhanced global ranking in tourist destinations, and positive media coverage can also reflect the success of the rebranding efforts.

The key to evaluating the effectiveness of rebranding lies in continuous monitoring and willingness to adapt. By establishing a robust system of feedback and analysis, CNMI can fine-tune its branding strategy, ensuring that it remains dynamic, relevant, and successful in attracting and satisfying tourists.

Navigating the complexities of rebranding the CNMI's tourism identity is a task fraught with challenges. Overcoming deep-rooted stereotypes and aligning with ever-changing global trends while preserving the unique essence of the islands demands a nuanced and sensitive approach.

The stereotypes that have long defined the CNMI as a quintessential sun-and-sand destination must be dismantled. This requires introducing fresh narratives that capture the islands' rich cultural fabric and diverse natural landscapes. Such a transformation in perception must be handled thoughtfully to engage new and existing audiences.

Moreover, adapting to the dynamic preferences of today's travelers is crucial. As travelers increasingly seek authentic experiences that allow for deeper connections with local culture and environment, the CNMI's rebranding efforts should cater to these evolving desires. However, this adaptation must not lead to losing the islands' unique character. The authenticity of the CNMI should be the cornerstone of its new brand identity.

Branding involving local communities, cultural experts, and historians can strike this delicate balance. Their insights will ensure that the rebranding is deeply rooted in the true ethos of the CNMI. Additionally, embracing sustainability and eco-consciousness in the brand narrative will align with the global shift towards environmental responsibility and conscious travel.

Furthermore, understanding the varied preferences and demographics of global travelers is essential. The CNMI must be agile in adjusting its marketing strategies to attract different traveler segments while maintaining a cohesive brand identity.

Therefore, rebranding CNMI's tourism sector requires a well-orchestrated strategy, balancing modern trends with traditional values. It involves a deep respect for the islands' heritage and a commitment to an authentic and sustainable tourism experience. Addressing these challenges with care and consideration will be pivotal in shaping a brand image that resonates with global travelers and remains true to CNMI's spirit.

Successfully rebranding the CNMI's tourism sector requires an ongoing commitment to evolution and responsiveness to the ever-changing global tourism landscape. Maintaining and refreshing the

CNMI's image over time is not just an option but a necessity for staying competitive and relevant.

Staying ahead in the fast-paced global tourism world means the CNMI must continually adapt its strategies to align with emerging trends and shifts in traveler behavior. This requires a keen understanding of global developments and an agile marketing and brand messaging approach. Such a strategy will preserve the CNMI's appeal to its current market and open doors to new audiences.

Regular market research is essential in this process. By keeping a finger on the pulse of changing trends, demographic shifts, and evolving expectations of tourists, the CNMI can adjust its branding efforts to resonate more strongly with its intended audience. This forward-thinking approach ensures that the CNMI remains ahead with a relevant and appealing tourism offering.

Periodically updating the brand image is crucial to maintain its relevance and appeal. This does not necessarily mean a complete rebranding but rather strategic updates to maintain the brand's freshness and engagement. Updating marketing materials, infusing new stories, or tweaking the visual elements are all part of keeping the brand dynamic and attractive.

Forging partnerships with industry influencers like travel bloggers and experts can inject new life into the branding strategy. These collaborations extend the reach of the CNMI's tourism sector to new audiences and bring innovative perspectives.

Central to these long-term branding strategies is the commitment to sustainability. With a growing global focus on eco-friendly and responsible tourism, integrating these aspects into the CNMI's brand is essential. This not only helps preserve the unique natural and cultural assets of the islands but also caters to the preferences of environmentally conscious travelers.

In summary, the CNMI's future in tourism branding hinges on its ability to remain flexible and responsive, continuously updating its image while staying rooted in its core values. By embracing innovation and keeping pace with global trends and traveler preferences, the CNMI can secure its place as an attractive and sustainable destination in the global tourism arena.

Reflecting on the rebranding and marketing efforts for CNMI, it becomes evident that the process is more than just superficial changes. It involves delving deep into the identity of the CNMI and facing the challenge of evolving in a competitive global tourism market while staying true to its roots. This endeavor demands a sensitive yet firm approach in striking a balance between preserving the islands' unique cultural and natural essence and meeting the shifting expectations of global travelers.

The steps taken to carve out a distinctive place for CNMI in the global tourism landscape, from integrating local values to executing comprehensive marketing strategies, lay a foundation. However, they also reveal the complexities and hurdles of such an undertaking. The involvement of local communities is crucial, yet it uncovers the intricate task of aligning diverse local interests with broader tourism goals.

However, this journey of destination branding is a continuous and challenging one. It does not end with a new logo or a marketing campaign; it demands constant vigilance and adaptation. As CNMI navigates this path, it is a stark reminder of the global tourism industry's relentless and often unforgiving nature. The experiences and strategies adopted by CNMI will be critical in maintaining its new image and facing the ongoing and future challenges of striving to stand out in a world of enticing destinations.

Chapter 19

Unleashing the Potential of Cultural Heritage in Tourism

In an era where global travel destinations often blur into a homogenous montage of beaches, hotels, and tourist traps, the CNMI stands at a pivotal crossroads. The challenge and opportunity lie in distinguishing itself through the rich tapestry of its cultural heritage, a facet of its identity that has been underplayed in its tourism narrative.

The cultural heritage of the CNMI is a rich amalgam of indigenous traditions and historical narratives, interwoven with various influences from throughout the Pacific region. This heritage offers more than just a window into the past; it presents an untapped potential to redefine and enrich the islands' tourism appeal. However, this treasure trove remains unexplored mainly, often overshadowed by the conventional allure of sun, sea, and sand.

The transition towards incorporating cultural heritage into the tourism landscape is not just about adding another attraction to the catalog. It represents a profound shift towards a more sustainable, meaningful, and authentic form of tourism. Such a transition can reshape perceptions, reinvigorate local economies, and foster a deeper understanding and respect for the CNMI's unique cultural identity.

The CNMI is a distinct cultural nexus where its history and customs are forged through native, colonial, and global influences.

However, the tourism industry has not wholly utilized this diverse cultural landscape.

Despite the wealth of cultural assets, the cultural role in the CNMI's tourism landscape has been somewhat limited. The dominant tourism model has primarily focused on the islands' natural beauty, particularly their stunning beaches and marine life, often overshadowing the cultural dimensions. While these natural attractions are undoubtedly valuable, they do not singularly define the CNMI experience.

This oversight in tapping into the full potential of cultural heritage in tourism has implications. It narrows the scope of what the CNMI can offer and risks undervaluing and underrepresenting the local cultures integral to the islands' identity. As global tourism trends evolve, with increasing numbers of travelers seeking authentic and culturally rich experiences, the CNMI's current approach may miss critical opportunities to attract a broader, more diverse visitor demographic.

Furthermore, this lack of emphasis on cultural heritage in tourism might contribute to a homogenized visitor experience, one that could be found in numerous other tropical destinations. By not fully integrating and showcasing its unique cultural identity, the CNMI risks being another stopover in the vast Pacific rather than a distinctive, must-visit location.

Therefore, reassessing the current state of cultural heritage in the CNMI's tourism sector is not only about preserving and honoring the past. It is about strategically positioning the islands for future success in a competitive global market, where the richness of cultural experience is increasingly becoming a key differentiator.

Focusing on cultural heritage in the tourism industry of the CNMI brings a spectrum of advantages, spanning economic growth, educational enrichment, and social empowerment. This strategy can significantly enhance the tourism experience in the CNMI, fostering a more sustainable and meaningful travel industry.

By spotlighting cultural heritage, the CNMI can stimulate its local economy in multiple ways. It opens up avenues for new businesses and services centered around cultural experiences, such as restaurants that offer Chamorro and Carolinian cuisine, traditional craft workshops, cultural education centers, or language schools to teach and preserve indigenous languages and traditions. These initiatives create employment opportunities and keep the economic benefits circulating within the community.

Moreover, a cultural heritage emphasis can diversify the CNMI's tourism offerings, making the economy more robust against market changes. Tourists drawn to cultural and heritage experiences often seek unique, in-depth encounters, potentially leading to more extended stays and increased spending. Thus, leveraging its unique cultural assets positions the CNMI to attract travelers who value and invest in authentic experiences.

Integrating cultural heritage into tourism also offers significant educational benefits. It cultivates a deeper understanding and respect for the CNMI's history and traditions among visitors, transforming a typical vacation into a journey of discovery. This focus on educational tourism can enhance global awareness and appreciation of the CNMI's distinct cultural identity, fostering international cultural exchange and understanding and helping dispel stereotypes.

Additionally, prioritizing cultural heritage in tourism reinforces community identity and pride. Interest from tourists in local heritage validates its importance and can instill pride among residents. This validation increases community involvement in preserving and promoting cultural traditions, aligning tourism with sustainable practices. When locals feel a sense of ownership and witness direct benefits from tourism, they are more inclined to care for and maintain their cultural sites and traditions.

In essence, emphasizing cultural heritage in the CNMI's tourism not only opens up economic diversification and strengthens the local economy but also plays a pivotal role in educating visitors and bolstering community identity. This approach charts a course towards a more sustainable, responsible, and enriching tourism sector that genuinely captures the essence of the islands.

Navigating the path of cultural heritage tourism in the CNMI involves addressing several challenges, particularly the delicate balance between preservation and commercialization, the effects of modernization and globalization, and the need to overcome stereotypes and misinterpretations.

The intersection of preservation and commercialization is a critical concern. On one hand, showcasing cultural heritage can enhance tourist engagement and economic gain. On the other hand, excessive commercialization risks diluting the authenticity of cultural experiences. This can lead to a superficial portrayal of traditions and potentially even exploitation of cultural resources. Therefore, the CNMI finds a balance where cultural heritage is accessible to tourists while maintaining its integrity and significance.

Modernization and globalization present another layer of complexity. These forces can erode traditional practices and values, leading to a loss of cultural identity. As the CNMI integrates into the global economy, there is a risk that unique cultural aspects may be overshadowed or altered to cater to a broader, more generic tourist audience. Guarding against the homogenization of culture requires conscious efforts to preserve traditional practices, languages, and customs.

Overcoming stereotypes and misinterpretations is also crucial. Tourists often arrive with preconceived notions about a destination and its culture, influenced by media portrayals or superficial understanding. These stereotypes can be damaging if they perpetuate myths or reduce a rich cultural heritage to a few token symbols. The CNMI must strive to present a nuanced and accurate representation of its culture, educating visitors on the depth and diversity of its traditions.

These challenges underscore the need for a thoughtful approach to cultural heritage tourism. Solutions might include:

- Developing guidelines for ethical and cultural representation,
- Investing in education and awareness programs for tourists and
- Involving local communities in decision-making processes.

By addressing these issues, the CNMI can ensure that its cultural heritage tourism contributes positively to its economy and upholds and celebrates the essence of its cultural identity.

Learning from global best practices and case studies can provide valuable insights for the CNMI in cultural heritage tourism. Examining how other destinations have successfully integrated their culture into their tourism offerings can offer a roadmap for the CNMI to follow.

One notable example comes from Kyoto, Japan, where the preservation of cultural heritage is seamlessly woven into the tourism experience (Kasuya, 2022). Kyoto showcases its rich history through well-preserved temples, traditional tea ceremonies, and Geisha culture. The city has managed to balance preserving its cultural integrity and accommodating tourists. This has been achieved by setting strict regulations to protect historical sites and engaging local communities in tourism activities, ensuring that the cultural experiences remain authentic.

Another successful case is seen in Bhutan, which has prioritized "high value, low impact" tourism (Zubiri, 2020). This approach focuses on offering quality experiences that deeply engage with Bhutanese culture while minimizing the negative impacts of tourism. The country imposes a daily fee on tourists, which is used to fund sustainable development projects, including cultural preservation. This model demonstrates how focusing on quality rather than quantity in tourism can enhance the visitor experience while benefiting the local community and preserving cultural heritage.

The CNMI can draw inspiration from these examples. Integrating cultural heritage into tourism does not just mean showcasing cultural sites and practices; it also involves ensuring that these experiences are sustainable, respectful, and beneficial to tourists and local communities. The CNMI can work towards developing tourism policies that emphasize protecting and promoting its unique cultural heritage while providing meaningful and immersive experiences for tourists.

Incorporating best practices from around the world involves understanding the local context and adapting these practices to fit the unique cultural landscape of the CNMI. It might involve developing community-based tourism initiatives where locals are directly involved in and benefit from tourism activities. Educational programs for tourists about local customs and traditions and ethical guidelines for experiencing and interacting with cultural sites and practices are also crucial.

By learning from these global examples and tailoring strategies to its context, the CNMI can establish itself as a leader in cultural heritage tourism, offering a tourism experience that is both enriching and respectful of its cultural legacy.

Enhancing the CNMI's tourism through cultural heritage requires a holistic approach that involves the community, respects authenticity, and leverages the expertise of cultural specialists. Involving local communities in the heart of tourism development ensures accurate cultural representation and directly brings economic benefits to those showcasing culture. This involvement could include community-led tours, cultural demonstrations, or local entrepreneurship, allowing for a more authentic and enriching tourist experience.

Simultaneously, it is imperative to represent the CNMI's culture responsibly. This means steering clear of stereotypes and offering a multifaceted view of the local customs, traditions, and lifestyle. Such representation should be handled with sensitivity and respect, always seeking consent from the community when using elements of their cultural heritage in tourism initiatives.

Collaboration with cultural experts and local artisans is also critical. These individuals offer essential perspectives and can enhance tourism experiences that are both engaging and informative. For instance, traditional craft workshops, cooking classes featuring local dishes, and guided tours of cultural sites can enhance the tourist experience. This collaboration also presents economic opportunities for local artisans, preserving traditional crafts and skills while providing them with a source of income.

Through these approaches, the CNMI can craft a tourism sector that showcases its rich cultural tapestry and supports and uplifts its local communities. This strategy results in a tourism experience that is authentic, responsible, and sustainable, benefiting both visitors and the local populace.

Crafting effective marketing strategies for CNMI's cultural heritage involves a careful blend of showcasing unique cultural elements and leveraging the reach of digital media. The emphasis in marketing should be on the rich, diverse cultural experiences that set the CNMI apart. Creating engaging content that tells the stories of the islands' traditions, history, and people is critical. This content can take various forms, such as immersive storytelling in brochures, dynamic websites, and compelling video narratives, offering a window into the CNMI's vibrant culture.

In the digital age, social media, travel blogs, and online forums are indispensable tools for reaching a global audience. These channels offer the perfect stage for promoting CNMI's cultural wealth. For instance, virtual tours, features on local artisans, and glimpses into cultural festivities can capture the interest of those planning their travels. Collaborations with travel influencers and bloggers focusing on cultural and sustainable tourism can also direct attention to the CNMI's unique offerings.

These digital avenues are promotional tools and facilitate interactive communication with potential tourists. They provide a space where travelers can engage, inquire, and even plan their visits, building anticipation and a connection with the CNMI's culture before their journey begins.

Through these tailored marketing efforts and the strategic use of digital platforms, the CNMI can highlight its cultural heritage, drawing in tourists seeking authentic, enriching travel experiences.

In the realm of cultural tourism, sustainable development is paramount. The CNMI must balance showcasing its rich cultural heritage and preserving it for future generations. This requires implementing sustainable practices that protect and honor cultural sites, traditions, and artifacts while offering enriching experiences for visitors.

One key aspect is carefully managing tourist footfall in culturally significant areas. Regulating visitor numbers, especially at sensitive sites, can prevent the wear and tear of high traffic, thereby preserving these locations' integrity. Additionally, educating tourists about local customs and respecting cultural sites helps maintain these treasures.

Moreover, integrating eco-friendly practices into cultural tourism is crucial. This might include using sustainable materials to construct and maintain tourism facilities or implementing waste reduction and recycling programs at cultural events and sites. These efforts protect the environment and resonate with a growing segment of travelers who prioritize sustainability in their choices.

By focusing on sustainable development, the CNMI can ensure that its cultural heritage remains a vibrant and integral part of its tourism offering, not just as a relic of the past but as a living, evolving part of its present and future.

The future of cultural heritage tourism in the CNMI is laden with opportunities, demanding a strategic and sensitive approach. To leverage its unique cultural identity in attracting tourists, the CNMI must carefully navigate between showcasing its rich heritage and ensuring sustainability.

Promising areas include organizing cultural festivals and events, offering vibrant platforms for tourists to engage with local traditions and arts, and supporting local artists and craftspeople. Such events enrich the tourist experience and help sustain the cultural ecosystem of the CNMI.

Another potential area is the development of guided cultural heritage trails or tours, where knowledgeable locals lead tourists through the islands' rich historical and cultural landscapes. These tours offer educational and meaningful experiences, connecting visitors with the CNMI's past.

A critical aspect of the long-term strategy is preserving cultural sites and artifacts, ensuring the continuity of the CNMI's cultural narrative, and providing a tangible link to the islands' heritage. Collaboration with educational institutions for research and documentation is vital in supporting this endeavor.

Educational initiatives aimed at locals and tourists are essential to foster a deeper appreciation and responsibility towards cultural heritage. This includes integrating cultural heritage into local education systems and creating informative visitor resources.

Ensuring local community involvement in developing and promoting cultural tourism is crucial. This approach enhances the authenticity of the tourist experience and ensures equitable sharing of the benefits of tourism, fostering a sustainable and inclusive model for cultural tourism.

The CNMI stands at a crossroads, with the potential to create a unique and enduring tourism experience by blending sustainable practices with a deep respect for its rich heritage. This approach will preserve the islands' cultural richness and offer a distinctive and memorable tourism experience.

In the CNMI, the intricate dance of preserving cultural integrity while promoting it as a tourism asset demands careful consideration and strategy. The responsibility falls on the shoulders of the tourism industry, local communities, cultural experts, and policymakers. Their collaborative efforts are essential in forging a tourism model that acknowledges and celebrates the islands' unique cultural identity.

This is a call to all involved in the CNMI's tourism industry to appreciate and utilize the full potential of cultural heritage. This involves crafting strategies that foster community participation, ensure respectful representation of local culture, and advocate for sustainable tourism practices. Such an approach promises economic prosperity, cultural enrichment, and social responsibility.

The path ahead is one of continuous engagement, learning, and cooperation. Stakeholders must maintain an open dialogue, share successful practices, and be open to innovative ideas. This cooperative approach is critical to evolving the CNMI's tourism industry in a way that honors its heritage, enhances its current state, and secures a sustainable future.

In wrapping up this chapter, it is clear that integrating cultural heritage into tourism in the CNMI is both a formidable task and a golden opportunity. It requires creativity, respect, and a profound commitment to the community's core values. By embarking on this path, the CNMI stands to create a model for cultural tourism that is economically viable, deeply meaningful, and sustainable.

Chapter 20

A New Horizon: Shaping a Sustainable and Equitable Future for CNMI Tourism

As the golden sun descends beneath the horizon, bathing the Northern Mariana Islands in its final glow of warmth, we observe the dawn of a transformative period for the region's tourism industry. The journey up to this moment, rich with learning and experience, has ushered us to the threshold of a new epoch - one where sustainability and equity are not mere concepts but the driving forces behind tourism. At the core of this epochal shift is a deep reverence for the islands' stunning natural landscapes and a commitment to preserving the rich tapestry of cultural heritage that makes CNMI an unparalleled destination.

This vision of a renewed tourism model is built on the foundations of collaboration, involving a symphony of voices from local communities, government entities, and international partners. It is about creating balance – managing the influx of visitors to protect fragile ecosystems and cultural sites, fostering eco-friendly accommodations that harmonize with the environment, and embracing renewable energy to power a greener tourism industry. Such strategic shifts are crucial in building a tourism sector resilient to the changing tides of time.

The soul of CNMI's tourism lies in the well-being and prosperity of its local communities. It is about creating pathways for empowerment – through educational initiatives that offer insights into sustainable tourism, providing employment opportunities that stem from an expanding tourism sector, and ensuring the active participation of locals in shaping the tourism narrative. Integrating the vibrant local festivals, arts, and culinary delights into the tourism experience enriches what CNMI offers. It kindles a sense of pride and economic empowerment among its people.

Innovation in tourism is pivotal in staying relevant in a rapidly evolving global landscape. It is about leveraging digital technology to craft immersive and interactive visitor experiences, from virtual tours that showcase the islands' beauty to digital platforms that offer deep dives into the rich cultural heritage of CNMI. Moreover, championing eco-conscious initiatives, like coral reef restoration and wildlife conservation, positions the islands as a beacon of eco-tourism, drawing in those seeking meaningful and mindful travel experiences.

Addressing the significant challenges brought about by climate change and economic instability requires a tourism model that's both resilient and flexible. Crafting a diverse range of tourism products, from adventure tourism to cultural excursions, and developing comprehensive disaster-preparedness plans are essential in shielding the industry from unforeseen shocks. In this context, resilience is about finding innovative ways to thrive amidst adversities.

As we stand at this critical juncture, contemplating the future of CNMI's tourism, our decisions today will sculpt the legacy we leave for generations. Opting for a path that prioritizes sustainable and equitable development is more than a choice – it is a commitment to preserving the islands' intrinsic beauty and cultural richness. This new horizon we envision is not just a hopeful dream; it is a practical, actionable roadmap leading to a future where CNMI's natural and cultural jewels are safeguarded and celebrated by everyone who steps onto its shores.

References

Aldred, J. (2008). Retrieved from https://www.theguardian.com/environment/2008/apr/22/renewableenergy.alternativeenergy

Alexander, E. (2019). Retrieved from https://www.harpersbazaar.com/uk/travel/g28936575/discovering-the-real-alberobello-the-home-of-puglias-enchanting-trulli/

Annan, K. (1999). Retrieved from https://www.un.org/sg/en/content/sg/articles/1999-11-29/help-third-world-help-itself

Azores Tourism. (2022). Retrieved from https://www.visitazores.com/en/sustainable-tourism-destination

Ballendorf, D. A., & Foster, S. (2021). Northern Mariana Islands. Retrieved from https://www.britannica.com/place/Northern-Mariana-Islands

Banton, C. (2022, June 8). Third World countries: Definition, criteria, and countries. Investopedia. https://www.investopedia.com/terms/t/third-world.asp

Britannica, T. Editors of Encyclopaedia. (2022, September 5). encomienda. Encyclopedia Britannica. https://www.britannica.com/topic/encomienda

Britannica, T. Editors of Encyclopaedia (2023, October 13). Third World. Encyclopedia Britannica. https://www.britannica.com/money/topic/Third-World

Cabrera, B. (2021). Retrieved from https://www.pacificislandtimes.com/post/the-cnmi-s-article-12-conundrum

Cassar, M. (2023). Retrieved from https://www.state.gov/reports/2023-investment-climate-statements/malta/

Chin, E. (2023). Retrieved from https://www.incorp.asia/blogs/what-makes-singapore-economy-tick-incorp-guide/

Commonwealth of the Northern Mariana Islands. (2023, March 22). https://www.doi.gov/oia/islands/cnmi

Davis, D., Kern-Allely, S., Muldoon, L., Tudela, J. M., Tudela, J., Raho, R., Pangelinan, H. S., Palacios, H., Tabaguel, J., Hinson, A., Lifoifoi, G., Villagomez, W., Fauver, J. R., Cash, H. L., Muña, E., Casey, S. T., & Khan, A. S. (2023). How the Commonwealth of the Northern Mariana Islands stalled COVID-19 for 22 months and managed its first significant community transmission. Western Pacific surveillance and response journal: WPSAR, 14(1), 1–10. https://doi.org/10.5365/wpsar.2023.14.1.965

Dietz, J. L. (1980). Dependency Theory: A Review Article [Review of Dependency and Development in Latin America; Mexican Agriculture 1521-1630: Transformation of the Mode of Production, by F. H. Cardoso, E. Faletto, & A. G. Frank]. Journal of Economic Issues, 14(3), 751–758. http://www.jstor.org/stable/4224952

Erediano, E. T. (2023, April 10). Transition report: Trip program misses Korea target. Marianas Variety News & Views. https://www.mvariety.com/news/transition-report-trip-program-misses-korea-target/article_4a04048a-d6da-11ed-a9cc-071fe8443efb.html

Esmores, K. B. (2022). Retrieved from https://www.saipantribune.com/featured/trip-japan-off-to-a-slow-start/article_fca4b83b-d97d-5a54-a74a-41feba7324fe.html

Esmores, K. E. B. (2022). Retrieved from https://www.saipantribune.com/featured/mva-seeks-additional-5m-for-trip-japan/article_5bc65160-25d5-5900-bfe3-fa09ed6a6d46.html

Farrell, D. A. (1991). History of the Northern Mariana Islands. (P. Koontz, Ed.). Public School System.

Fish and Wildlife Service, Interior. (2005). Retrieved from https://www.federalregister.gov/documents/2005/01/06/05-240/endangered-and-threatened-wildlife-and-plants-mariana-fruit-bat-pteropus-mariannus-mariannus

Fisheries, N. (2023). Retrieved from https://www.fisheries.noaa.gov/pacific-islands/endangered-species-conservation/marine-protected-species-mariana-islands#more-information

Foster, S. and Ballendorf, Dirk Anthony (2023, November 17). Northern Mariana Islands. Encyclopedia Britannica. https://www.britannica.com/place/Northern-Mariana-Islands

Frąckiewicz, M. (2023). Retrieved from https://ts2.space/en/the-intersection-of-drones-and-tourism-in-rwanda-a-new-perspective/#gsc.tab=0

Fritz, G. (2001). The Chamorro: A history and ethnography of the Mariana Islands. (E. Craddock, Trans., S. Russell, Ed.) (2nd ed.). Division of Historic Preservation.

Grecni, Z., Derrington, E. M., Greene, R., Miles, W., & Keener, V. (2021). (rep.). Climate Change in the Commonwealth of the Northern Mariana Islands: Indicators and Considerations for Key Sectors. Honolulu, Hi: Report for the Pacific Islands Regional Climate Assessment. file:///Users/tatianab/Downloads/climate-change-in-cnmi-pirca-2021-lo-res%20(1).pdf

Hayes, A. (2023). Retrieved from https://www.investopedia.com/terms/a/augmented-reality.asp

Heath, L. (1975). Education for Confusion: A Study of Education in the Mariana Islands 1688-1941. The Journal of Pacific History, 10(1), 20–37. http://www.jstor.org/stable/25168207

Hezel, F. X. (1988). From Conquest to Colonization: Spain in the Marianas 1690-1740. Micronesian Seminar. https://micsem.org/article/from-conquest-to-colonization-spain-in-the-marianas-1690-1740/

HotelMinder. (2023). Retrieved from https://www.hotelminder.com/smart-hotels-everything-you-need-to-know

Kaefer, F. (2016, September 6). Origins and success of 100% pure New Zealand destination brand. https://placebrandobserver.com/origins-success-pure-new-zealand-destination-brand/

Kasuya, N. (2022). Kyoto. Retrieved December 6, 2023, from World Bank website: https://www.worldbank.org/en/programs/tokyo-development-learning-center/partnership/kyoto

Kenton, W. (2023). Retrieved from https://www.investopedia.com/terms/w/web-20.asp

Koteshov, D. (2023). Retrieved from https://anywhere.epam.com/business/artificial-intelligence-in-tourism-and-travel-industry

Laird, L. M. (2003). Retrieved from https://www.sciencedirect.com/science/article/abs/pii/B012227430X004748

Limol, K.-A. E. (2022). Retrieved from https://www.mvariety.com/news/15-million-in-arpa-funds-spent-on-japan-tourism-market/article_0ce73836-2cd2-11ed-93bb-67f7c158d2be.html

Lindstrom, L. amont. (n.d.). Retrieved from https://www.everyculture.com/To-Z/Vanuatu.html

Lowatcharin, G., & Stallmann, J. I. (2016). Centralized and Decentralized Policy System: A Cross-National Mixed-Methods Study of the Effects of Policing Structures with Lessons for Thailand (dissertation). Columbia, MO.

manatuscostarica.com. (2019). Retrieved from https://manatuscostarica.com/blog/manatus-tortuguero-where-sustainable-tourism-thrives/

Marianas Visitors Authority. (2006, May 9). Celebrating 30 years of tourism: The beginning. Saipan Tribune. https://www.saipantribune.com/index.php/a715ef9f-1dfb-11e4-aedf-250bc8c9958e/

Maurin, I. (2020). Retrieved from https://www.saipantribune.com/news/local/saving-our-corals-eyes-of-the-reef-marianas/article_fd289

Maurin, I. (2020). Retrieved from https://www.saipantribune.com/news/local/saving-our-corals-eyes-of-the-reef-marianas/article_fd2891c0-1169-518f-be92-32cc52887253.html

Munford, M. (2016). Retrieved from https://www.forbes.com/sites/montymunford/2016/12/21/silicon-valletta-accelerates-maltas-emerging-tech-hub-in-the-mediterranean/?sh=5b60f1a533ef

MVA. (2021). Retrieved from https://www.saipantribune.com/news/local/marianas-tourism-resumption-investment-plan-launched/article_c75a4119-07d5-5d04-ada3-553623c57de6.html

NMI Museum. (2023). Retrieved from https://nmimuseum.org/the-german-period/

NMI Museum. (2023). Retrieved from https://nmimuseum.org/the-spanish-period/

National Park Service. (2005). Retrieved from https://www.nps.gov/parkhistory/online_books/wapa/adhi/adhi1.htm

Outlook Publishing. (2023). Retrieved from https://issuu.com/outlookpublishing/docs/vanuatu-travel-guide-2023

PATA. (2023). Retrieved from https://www.pata.org/blog/kiribati-recognises-the-value-in-sustainable-regenerative-tourism

Rosenfeld, K. (Ed.). (2023). How the Galapagos Islands is a model for sustainable, responsible travel. Retrieved from https://www.travelagewest.com/Travel/Central-South-America/how-is-the-Galapagos-sustainable

Sheldon, R. (2022). Retrieved from https://www.techtarget.com/whatis/definition/virtual-reality

Simmons, J. (n.d.). Retrieved from https://www.responsiblevacation.com/copy/overtourism-in-venice

Spector, J. (2023). Retrieved from https://www.canarymedia.com/articles/clean-energy/kauai-is-a-clean-energy-leader-its-secret-a-publicly-owned-grid

Staf, P. I. T. N. (2021). Retrieved from https://www.pacificislandtimes.com/post/cnmi-to-subsidize-airlines-hotels-and-tour-agencies-to-jumpstart-tourism

Sustain Europe. (2021). Iceland: Where beauty and sustainability go hand in hand. Retrieved from https://www.sustaineurope.com/iceland-where-beauty-and-sustainability-go-hand-in-hand-20211002.html

Tamplin, T. (2023). Retrieved from https://www.financestrategists.com/wealth-management/blockchain/blockchain-in-tourism/

Tan, Aleck Danielle. (June 2020). Manila galleons in the Commonwealth of the Northern Mariana Islands: An analysis of the cultural impacts on Santa Margarita and Nuestra Senora De La Concepcion (Master's Thesis, East Carolina University). Retrieved from the Scholarship. (http://hdl.handle.net/10342/8598.)

The Adept Traveler. (2023). Retrieved from https://adept.travel/destinations/tongatapu-tonga

The Druk Journal. (2019). Retrieved from https://www.tourism.gov.bt/uploads/attachment_files/tcb_jJocRL3Q_The%20Druk%20Journal%2010.pdf

Tolentino, D. (2023). Retrieved from https://www.guampedia.com/mannakhilo-and-mannakpapa/#:~:text=Previously%2C%20traditional%20CHamoru%20society%20was,of%20the%20lower%20class%20manachang.

Tourism Fiji. (2023). Retrieved from https://www.fiji.travel/articles/8-unique-cultural-experiences-you-must-do-in-fiji

Tourism New Zealand, & Skift. (2018). Retrieved from https://skift.com/2018/09/19/how-new-zealands-unique-approach-to-hospitality-drives-group-and-incentive-travel/

Twining-Ward, L. (2002). Retrieved from https://iucn2.cnr.ncsu.edu/images/9/9e/T20224_Twining-Ward.pdf

U.S. Department of Agriculture. (n.d.). Retrieved from https://www.nal.usda.gov/farms-and-agricultural-production-systems/hydroponics

USINDOPACOM Joint Operational Law Team (J (Ed.). (2023). Retrieved from https://www.pacom.mil/LinkClick.aspx?fileticket=UUf_gsxkuPQ%3d&portalid=55

Utomo, D. (2020). Retrieved from https://www.timeout.com/singapore/news/nparks-launches-a-real-time-map-where-you-can-monitor-crowd-levels-at-singapores-parks-040520

van den Bossche, P. L. H. (2008). NGO Involvement in the WTO: A Comparative Perspective. Journal of International Economic Law, 11, 717-749. https://doi.org/10.1093/jiel/jgn032

Vogt, S. R., & Williams, L. L. (2004). Common Flora & Fauna of the Mariana Islands (1st ed.). Laura R. Williams & Scott R. Vogt.

Wear, A. (2020). Retrieved from https://reasonstobecheerful.world/the-island-where-everyone-owns-the-wind/

Wusinich-Mendez, D., & Trappe, C. (Eds.). (2007). (rep.). Report on the Status of Marine Protected Areas in Coral Reef Ecosystems of the United States (Vol. 1). Silver Spring, MD: NOAA Technical Memorandum CRCP 2.

Zubiri, S. (2020, May 13). "Authentic" travel experiences are hard to find — but not in this country. Retrieved December 6, 2022, from CNBC website: https://www.cnbc.com/2020/05/13/travel-to-bhutan-an-authentic-experience-in-asia.html

www.ingramcontent.com/pod-product-compliance
Lightning Source LLC
Chambersburg PA
CBHW070143100426
42743CB00013B/2809